Women Respond to the Men's Movement

A FEMINIST COLLECTION

Kay Leigh Hagan, *Editor*
Foreword by Gloria Steinem

HarperSanFrancisco
A Division of HarperCollins*Publishers*

WOMEN RESPOND TO THE MEN'S MOVEMENT: *A Feminist Collection*.
Copyright © 1992 by Kay Leigh Hagan. All rights reserved. Printed
in the United States of America. No part of this book may be used
or reproduced in any manner whatsoever without written permission except in the case of brief quotations embodied in critical articles and reviews. For information address HarperCollins Publishers,
10 East 53rd Street, New York, NY 10022.

TEXT DESIGN BY CHRISTY BUTTERFIELD

FIRST EDITION

Library of Congress Cataloging-in-Publication Data

Women respond to the men's movement: a feminist collection / Kay
    Leigh Hagan, editor. — lst ed.
        p.   cm.
    ISBN 0–06–250996–9
        1. Men's movement—United States.   2. Feminist criticism
    —United States.   I. Hagan, Kay Leigh.
    HQ1090.3.W66   1992   91–59031
    305.32—dc20   CIP

92 93 94 95 96 ❖ HAD 10 9 8 7 6 5 4 3 2 1

This edition is printed on acid-free and recycled paper that meets the
American National Standards Institute Z39.48 Standard.

Contents

Foreword

 *Gloria Steinem*

MAKE NO MISTAKE about it: Women want a men's movement. We are literally dying for it. If you doubt that, just listen to women's desperate testimonies of hope that the men in our lives will become more nurturing toward children, more able to talk about emotions, less hooked on a spectrum of control that extends from not listening through to violence, and less repressive of their own human qualities that are called "feminine"—and thus suppressed by cultures in which men dominate.

If this anecdotal evidence isn't enough, consider some random facts:

- One in four women is sexually assaulted in her lifetime, and not usually by a stereotypical criminal. In one recent survey, 51 percent of college men said they would rape if they could get away with it.

- Domestic violence is the single largest cause of injury to women in the United States. The most dangerous place for a woman is not in the street but in her own home. More than half of battering husbands also abuse their children.

- Battered women are most likely to be killed after an attempt to escape; yet 40 percent of women who apply for shelters for themselves and their children can't find room because such programs are low on the list of tax priorities for male-dominated legislatures.

- One in four female college students experiences rape or at-
tempted rape, and 84 percent know their attackers, but only
5 percent have enough faith in the system—or belief that it
wasn't somehow "their fault"—to report it to the police.

- According to a study done by the organization 9-to-5 even
before the Thomas-Hill hearings had educated the country on
this issue, about half of women in the paid labor force had
experienced some form of sexual harassment.

- Among those divorced men who seek custody of their children, about 70% are successful, often due to their greater
earning ability, better chances of remarrying, or to judges'
unwillingness to believe sexual abuse charges brought by a
mother and testified to by a child—and this remains true
even when there is medical evidence of such child abuse.

- The single most common occasion for female homicide is not
robbery, gangs, or drugs, but an argument with a man.

- Even where there is a concern for men of color—for instance, the current move to create all-male schools so that
African-American boys will have role models—there is rarely
an equal concern for girls.

As Donna Britt recently wrote in an essay in the *Washington Post*
"What About the Sisters?":

> *Who's worried about the mounting numbers of black women
> raising their kids alone; and those getting the life knocked out
> of them by angry, frustrated brothers? Who supports career
> women, whose difficulties with being black and female in an
> often-hostile work world are denigrated by certain black
> men—who suggest each sister's success is bought at a brother's
> expense? How about the myriad guys who suggest that while
> racism is real, sexism is a frivolous, white-girl notion?*

As Britt points out, even when black women have jobs, their earning power is far less than that of employed black men (and somewhat less than that of white women), yet they are solely responsible for 54 percent of the nation's black children.

Remember such facts when you read the mix of skepticism and hope in the voices gathered here. We both want to believe in male change, and have little reason to do so. Remember, too, that women experience more subtle versions of men's distance from nurturing and empathic roles; for instance, the killing double burden of working in and outside the home that has always been a fact of life for poor women is now one for middle-class women, as well. Perhaps the psychic leap of twenty years ago, *Women can do what men can do*, must now be followed by, *Men can do what women can do*.

In short, the question we must ask—and both men and women must keep asking—is not why women can't escape male violence, but why men do it. Is the men's movement uprooting the politics of patriarchy, or just giving them a new face?

To the nuances of our answer, each of us brings our own unique experience within the politics of this culture. We must be conscious of that. For instance: I'm more optimistic about men's willingness and ability to change—and also about their enlightened self-interest in doing so—because I happened to have a nurturing father. Since he made a living as an itinerant antique dealer who worked out of home and car, he could take the place of my mother, who was often ill. Not only did my father make clear that he enjoyed my company in his vagabond travels, but both my parents believed that children should be respected, never hit or humiliated. That's a very different experience from what seems to be the norm: growing up with a father made to seem distant by society's work pattern if nothing else, or one who treats daughters in some differential way that varies from benign neglect to seduction and abuse. On the other hand, I also grew up seeing evidence of a male-dominant culture all around me, from women so deprived of self-esteem and attention that they sometimes bragged about their husbands' violent rages, to the assumption of my male classmates that caring for home and children could never be their proper concern.

Perhaps this wide range in my own life is why I see such diversity under the umbrella of what might be called the men's movement. I know longtime allies like John Stoltenberg, author of *Refusing to Be a Man,* and such pioneering projects as the New York school program that delighted sixth-grade boys by teaching them to care for babies (reported in *Ms.* and a television special as "Oh Boy, Babies!"). I also know tried-and-true groups like the Oakland Men's Project, which for thirteen years has acted on the motto "Men's Work: To Stop Male Violence." It not only provides nonviolent male role models and strategies to boys in the East Bay, but has also created a community of men of different races, ethnicities, and sexualities who provide for each other the kind of support and intimacy usually found only in women's groups. Furthermore, just this week, I met a new group in Manchester, Vermont, whose members—white and mostly middle class, like that community itself—were surprised to find that not one of them was interested in the atavistic "masculine" values proposed by Robert Bly in *Iron John.* No matter how scary and new, they wanted to explore their "feminine" side and thus their androgynous potential as whole human beings.

At the other end of the spectrum, I've encountered "father's rights" groups that support men's custody cases without regard to evidence of sexual abuse, condemn the reporting of facts like those in this foreword as "male bashing," and insist that men are oppressed as "wimps" (or "success objects," as Warren Farrell says). That's no more (and no less) true than saying white Americans are oppressed by racism. As for Robert Bly, though he seems to have started out with some idea that men should explore the full circle of human qualities within themselves, perhaps like Freud, whose testimony to childhood sexual abuse was so unpopular that he presented it as children's wishful thinking instead—Bly seems to have returned to the easier sell of old warlike language of kings and battles, closeness only to males and measuring adulthood by men's distance from mothers, thus reconstructing patriarchy albeit in a supposedly gentler form.

We have to use our own good instincts when deciding what among this diversity to trust, learn from, and nourish. We need to ask questions. For instance, does the group (or book, or person)

- use atavistic words of hierarchy and warfare instead of new language that breaks down boundaries between women and men?

- make us feel safer as women?

- make men feel more able to cross boundaries of homophobia, racism, class, and distance from women (including mothers)?

- include activism that puts money and time where its principles are, especially with the diminishing of violence?

- perhaps most of all, encourage men to take responsibility for nurturing children?

When the answer to these questions is yes or even trying hard to be yes, then women can find allies in a shared struggle toward a new future.

After all, if it's fair to say that there is more virtue where there is more choice, then men who choose to reject male privilege may be more virtuous than the rest of us. They will earn our trust. They will also discover the full circle of human qualities within themselves.

The truth is this: For both women and men, completing our full circle lies in the direction we have not been.

Gloria Steinem is a cofounder of Ms. Magazine *and is now its consulting editor. She travels widely as a feminist organizer and speaker. Her most recent book is* Revolution from Within: A Book of Self-Esteem.

Introduction

🔥 *Kay Leigh Hagan*

OVER A YEAR ago, my mother enclosed in a letter a newspaper comic strip poking gentle fun at the burgeoning men's movement. Known for having a strong opinion on virtually any subject, she'd written her response in the margin. "The men's movement should have started twenty years ago," she said. "Maybe someday they will look 'inside' to understand." Her comment reflected the hope and cynicism that resonate with many women as we encounter this phenomenon, the men's movement.

What *do* we think and feel about the men's movement? Is it a movement toward a society of mutual respect and safety for all, or just propaganda for a "kinder, gentler patriarchy"—or both? I've heard women respond in many ways—from cautious hope that men are coming to terms with the realities of true partnership and shared power, to utter disgust at the "chorus of whining white men," to deep-rooted fear that the men's movement has only legitimized a fashionable new form of woman-hating. Some women are confused by the onslaught of stylized media coverage, which hails the movement as the next great influence on society while simultaneously lambasting it with ridicule through cartoons, sitcom jokes, and sarcasm. Other women, out of the media loop by chance or by choice, profess to know nothing about it. Still others are encountering the men's movement primarily through male companions, deeply affected by the current plethora of books and workshops on the subject.

At a regional booksellers' convention last fall, on the evening after watching Anita Hill's testimony, I happened to share a banquet table with the author of a book popular with the mythopoetic branch of the men's movement. Our lively conversation moved from comparing notes on our respective books, to the Thomas hearings, to the general state of affairs between women and men, then to the film *Thelma and Louise*. Looking prudish and smug, the author said he'd refused to see *Thelma and Louise* and added, after a practiced pause, "Twenty years of male-bashing is enough."

My response was an uncharacteristic speechlessness (in this regard, I take after my mother, rarely hesitating to voice my opinion), and I suspect we were both relieved at the timely arrival of dinner. But his remark haunted me. We are of the same generation, race, and probably class, both writing books with the aim of helping people come to a deeper understanding of themselves and society. Surely our similarities outweigh our differences. I felt outrage, fear, and curiosity. What is really going on in this men's movement? As I began to pay closer attention, I found that his attitude was, of course, just one expression of a "movement" that has many faces. A month later, when asked to edit a feminist collection of women's responses to the men's movement, I found the opportunity irresistible.

For feminists, the phenomenon of men organizing on behalf of themselves as men in a society that is—for the most part—defined and controlled by men, holds a certain curious irony. Although I communicate regularly with many feminist thinkers, writers, and activists in the course of my work, early on no one I knew was particularly interested in these gatherings of mostly white men affirming primal masculinity in expensive workshops. With an arctic backlash plunging the social climate into a sexist deep-freeze unprecedented in memory, the idea of a men's movement was in fact so absurd as to be amusing, and served to provide a needed bit of comic relief. But as the gatherings gained popularity, enchanted the media, and assumed their context in the year's events, this men's movement took on a different meaning, one that called for serious scrutiny. By the time I issued a request for contributions to this collection in December 1991, the response from feminists was immediate and passionate. Even women unable to participate sent their enthusiastic support for the book, calling it needed and important. It is time, they agreed, for feminists to share our views on the men's movement.

At another moment in history, the phenomenon of a men's movement might have passed through the culture largely unnoticed. Gatherings where "men talk to men about men" are nothing if not ordinary in our society, as Kathleen Carlin observes. Times of great change, however, can cause ordinary events to take on extraordinary significance. The growing resistance to women's social and political gains over the past twenty years, well documented in Susan Faludi's lucid best-seller *Backlash,* created a setting in which this men's movement came to symbolize in part the awkward transition from one value system to another—what Riane Eisler describes as a shift from the values of domination to those of partnership.

Such a fundamental shift in the social order leaves no one unaffected. Faced with the daily realities of sharing power with women at home, at work, and in the community, many men have found in the men's movement a place to explore and express dissatisfaction with their changing social position, and confusion about their identities as men. Robert Bly's book *Iron John: A Book About Men,* selling over a half-million copies and representing the mythopoetic stance, helped to galvanize public opinion on the subject during the past year, along with the Gulf War, the film *Thelma and Louise,* the Clarence Thomas hearings, and the William Kennedy Smith trial. This succession of events stimulated unprecedented public discussion about gender, power, and privilege, and continues to be the focus of many heated conversations as we talk with each other about the impact these things have on the practical aspects our daily lives. Confronted with these events, we must think deeply about things that usually remain just below consciousness, parts of the silent infrastructure at the core of the dominant culture.

In this age of technological impatience, we are not trained to think deeply, but to receive information and process our thoughts in sound bytes, headlines, and sitcoms. The intellectual structure of feminism encourages us to be intelligent skeptics, to investigate beyond the superficial images constructed for us by the media. In all its varieties, feminism views *interconnection* as important: war, incest, pollution, racism, poverty, and how men treat women are not separate from each other, but integrally linked in a larger value system. Feminism asks us to look always for the subtle linkages that connect one thing to another, as well as the reversals that serve to distract us from the issues of our greatest concern.

This book is an exercise in such critical thinking, the kind of thinking that is tough, compassionate, fearless, and essential to self-determination. The essays collected here explore the connections and reversals, both obvious and obscured, that help us understand the depth, complexity, and implications of the men's movement. In the tradition of feminism, you will find personal stories describing women's experiences, questions that challenge the status quo, insights that crack the veneer of media, and concrete suggestions for practicing gender justice in our daily lives.

My own response to the men's movement has changed as a result of editing this book. Although my cynicism is not unfounded, I find evidence here to support my fragile hope for a society where women and men live and work as respectful allies to heal the planet. May this book be a useful tool toward that end.

Kay Leigh Hagan
Friday, March 13, 1992
Waxing Moon

Kay Leigh Hagan is a workshop leader and the author of two books: Internal Affairs: A Journalkeeping Workbook for Self-Intimacy *and* Prayers to the Moon: Exercises in Self-Reflection. *She is the creator of* Fugitive Information, *a subscription series of interactive feminist essays.*

Women
Respond
to the Men's
Movement

Nicole Hollander

Nicole Hollander is the creator of the syndicated cartoon strip
Sylvia. *Her latest book is* Tales from the Planet Sylvia.

Limberlost

Ursula K. Le Guin

THE POET REVOLVED slowly counterclockwise in the small, dark, not very deep pool. The novelist sat on the alder log that dammed the creek to make the pool. Also on the log were the poet's clothes, except his underpants. Coming upstream to the swimming hole, they had passed a naked nut-brown maid, beached and frontal to the sun; but she was young and they were not; and the poet was not Californian. "You don't mind if I'm old-fashioned about modesty?" he had asked, disarmingly. The novelist, although a Californian, did not mind. The poet's massive body was impressive enough as it was. Age, slacking here and tightening there what had been all smooth evenness in youth, gave pathos and dignity to that strong beast turning in the dark water. Among roots and the dark shadows of the banks, the hands and arms shone white. The novelist's bare feet, though tanned, also gleamed pallid under the water, as she sat rather less than comfortably on the log, wondering whether she should have pulled off shirt and jeans and joined the poet in his pool. She had been at his conference less than an hour and did not know the rules.

Did he want a companion, or a spectator? Did it matter? She splashed the water with her feet and deplored her inability to do, to know, what she wanted herself—fifty-five years old and sitting in adolescent paralysis, a bump on a log. Should I swim? I don't want to. I want to. Should I? Which underpants am I wearing? This is like the first day of summer camp. I want to go home. I ought to swim. Ought I? Now?

The poet spared her further debate by hauling out on the far end of the log. He was shivering. The log was in sunlight, but the air was cool. Discovering that he would not soon get dry in wet boxer shorts, he did then remove them, but very modestly, back turned, sitting down again quickly. He spread his underpants out on the log to dry, and conversed with his guest.

An expansive gesture as he described the events of the first week of the conference swept his socks into the water. He caught one, but the current took the other out of reach. It sank slowly. He mourned; the novelist commiserated. He dismissed the sock.

"The Men have raised a Great Phallus farther up the river," he said, smiling. "It was their own idea. I'd show you, but it's off limits to the Women. A temenos. Very interesting, some of the ritual that has developed this week! I am hearing men talk—not sports scores and business, but talk—"

Impressed and interested, the novelist listened, trying to ignore a lesser fascination: the sock. It had reemerged, all the way across the sun-flecked water, under a muddy, rooty bank. It was now moving very slowly but apparently—yes—definitely clockwise in a circle that would bring it back toward the log. The novelist sought and found a broken branch and held it ready, idly teasing the water with it. Housewife, she thought, ashamed. Fixated on socks. Prose writer!

The poet, sensitive and alert even when talking of his concerns, observed, and asked what she was fishing for.

"Your sock is coming back," she said.

In a silence of complete fellow feeling, they both watched the stately progress of the floating sock, coming round unhurried in the fullness of time, astronomically certain, till the current brought it within branch reach. It was lifted dripping on the forked end. In quiet triumph the novelist turned the branch to the poet, presenting the sock to its owner, who removed it from the branch and squeezed it thoughtfully.

Soon after this he dressed, and they returned downstream to the conference center and the scattered cabins under the redwoods.

The food was marvelous. Infinitely imaginatively vegetarian, eclectic but not hodgepodge: the chilis hot, the salads delicate, the curries fragrant. The kitchen staff who produced these wonders were unlike the other people at the conference, though in fact several of them were members of the conference working out their fees. When they came out front and listened to the lecture on the Hero, they disappeared into the others and she could not recognize them; but in the crowded, hot, flashing kitchen, each of them seemed almost formidably individual, laughing more than anyone else here, talking differently, moving with deft purpose, so that the onlooker felt superfluous and inferior, not because the cooks meant to impress or to exclude but only because, being busy with the work in hand, they were quite unconscious of doing so.

After dinner on the second day, in honey-colored evening sunlight, crossing the broad wooden bridge across the creek between the main hall and her set of cabins, the novelist stopped and set her hands on the rough railing. I have been here before! I know this creek, this bridge, that trail going up into the trees— Such moments were a familiar accompaniment to tension and self-consciousness. She had felt them waiting to be asked to dance in dancing class at twelve, and at fifty in a hotel room in a city she had never seen before. Sometimes they justified themselves as a foresight remembered, bringing with them a queer double-exposure effect of that place where she had foreseen being in this place. But this time the experience was one of pure recognition, unexplainable but not uncanny, though solemnified by the extraordinary grandeur of the setting.

For the creek ran and the path led from fog-softened golden light into a darkness under incredible trees. It was always dark under them, and silent, and bare, for their huge community admitted little on a smaller scale. In the open clearings weeds and brambles and birds and bugs made the usual lively mess and tangle; under the big trees the flash of a scrub jay's wing startled as it would in the austere reaches of a Romanesque church. To come under the trees was as definite a transition as entering a building, but a building the size of a county.

Yet in among those immense living trunks there were also some black, buttressed objects that confused the sense of scale still further, for though squat, they were bigger than the cabins—much bigger. In bulk and girth, they were bigger than the trees. They were ruins. Tree ruins, the logged and burned-over stumps of the original forest. With effort, the novelist comprehended that the sequoias so majestically towering their taper bulk and gracile limbs all around here were second growth, not even a century old, mere saplings, shoots, scions of the great presences that had grown here in a length of silence now altogether and forever lost.

All the same, it was very quiet under the trees, and still quieter at night. There were refinements of the absence of sound, which the novelist had never before had the opportunity to observe. The cabins of her group straggled along, one every ten or twenty yards, unlighted, above the creek, which ran shallow but almost soundless, as if obeying the authority of the redwoods, their counsel of silence. There was no wind. Fog would mosey in over the hills from the sea before dawn to hush what was hushed already. Far away one small owl called once. Later, one mosquito shrilled hopelessly for a moment at the screen.

The novelist lay in darkness on her narrow board bunk in her sleeping bag listening to nothing and wondering if this was the bag her daughter had been using when she got the flu camping last summer and how long flu germs might live in the dark, warm, moist medium of a zippered sleeping bag. Her thoughts ran on such matters because she was acutely uncomfortable. Sometimes she thought it was diarrhea, sometimes a bladder infection, sometimes a coward spirit. Whatever it was, would it force her yet again to leave the germy warmth of the sleeping bag and take her flashlight and try to find the evasive path up that ominous hiss to the all too communal, doorless, wet-floored toilets, praying that nobody would join her in her misery? Yes. No, maybe not. She heard a screen door creak, a cabin or two downstream, and almost immediately after, a soft, rushing noise: a man pissing off his cabin porch onto the dark, soft, absorbent ground of redwood leaf and twig and bark. O lucky Men, who need not crouch and straddle! Her bladder twinged, remorseless. "I do not have to go pee," she told herself, unconvinced. "I am not sick." She listened to the terrific silence. Nothing lived. But there, deep in the hollow darkness, a soft, lively sound: a little fart. And, now that she was all ears, presently another fart, louder, from a cabin on higher ground. The beans with chilis would probably explain it. Or did it need explanation, did people like cattle add nightly to the methane in the atmosphere, had those who had slept in longhouses by this creek been accustomed to this soft concert? For it was pleasing, almost melodious, this sparse pattern of a snore here—a long efflatus there—a little sigh—against the black and utter stillness.

When she was nearly asleep, she heard voices far upstream, male voices, chanting, as if from the dawn of history. Deep, primeval. The Men were performing the rituals of manhood. But the little farts in the night were nearer and dearer.

The Women sat in a circle on the sand, about thirty of them. Nearby the shallow river widened to the sea. Soft, fog-paled sunshine of the north coast lay beautifully on low breakers and dunes. The Women passed an ornamented wooden wand from hand to hand; who held the wand, spoke; the others listened. It did not seem quite right to the novelist. A good thing, but not the right one. Men wanted wands, women did not, she thought. These women had dutifully accepted the wand, but left to themselves they might have preferred some handwork and sat talking round and about like a flock of sparrows. Sparrows are disorderly, don't take turns, don't shut up to listen to the one with the wand, peck and talk at the same time. The wind blew softly, the wand passed. A woman in her twenties who wore an emblem of carved wood and feathers on a chain round her neck read a manuscript poem in a trembling voice half lost in the distant sound of the breakers. "My arms are those wings," she read, her voice shaken by fear and passion till it broke. The wand passed. A blond, fine-boned woman in her forties spoke of the White Goddess, but the novelist had ceased to listen, nervously rehearsing what she would say, should she say it? should she not? The wand passed to her. "It seems to me, coming in from outside, into the middle of this, you know, just for a couple of days, but perhaps just because of that I can be useful, anyhow it seems to me that to some extent some of the women here are sort of looking for a, for something actually to sort of *do*. Instead of kind of talking mostly in a sort of derivative way," she said in a harsh, chirping voice like a sparrow's. Shaking, she passed the wand. After the circle broke up, several women told her with enthusiasm about the masked dancing last Wednesday night, when the Women had acted out the female archetype of their choice. "It got wild," one said cheerfully. Another woman told her that this leader of the Women had quarreled with that one and personalities were destroying harmony. Several of them started making a large dragon out of wet sand, and while doing so told her that this year was different from earlier years, before the Men and the Women were separated, and that the East Coast meetings were always more spiritual than the West Coast meetings, or vice versa. They all chattered till the Men came back from their part of the beach, some with faces marked splendidly with charcoal.

The fine-boned blond whom the novelist had not listened to rode beside her in the car going back inland, a long, rough road through the logged-out coast range. "I've been coming to this place all my life," she said with a laugh. "It was a summer camp. I started coming when I was ten. Oh, it was wonderful then! I still meet people who came to Limberlost."

"Limberlost!" said the novelist.

"It was Camp Limberlost," said the other woman, and laughed again, affectionately.

"But I went there," said the novelist. "I went to Camp Limberlost. You mean this is it? Where the conference is? But I was wondering, earlier this year, I realized I had no idea where it was, or how to find out. I didn't know where it was when I went there. It was in the redwoods, that's literally all I knew. We all got into a bus downtown, and talked for six hours, you know, and then we were there—you know how kids are, they don't *notice*—but it was a Girl Reserve camp then. The YW ran it. I had to join the Girl Reserves to come."

"The city took it over after the war," the other woman said, her eyes merry and knowing. "This really is it. This is Limberlost."

"But I don't remember it," the novelist said in distress.

"The conference is in the old Boys Camp. The Girls Camp was upstream about a mile. Maybe you never came down here."

Yes. The novelist remembered that Jan and Dorothy had cut Camp Fire one evening and sneaked out of camp and down the creek to Boys Camp. They had hidden across the creek behind stumps and shrubs in the twilight, they had hooted and bleated and meowed until the Boys began coming out of their cabins, and then a counselor had come out, and Jan and Dorothy had run away, and got back after dark, muddy and triumphant, madly giggling in the jammed cabin after Lights Out, reciting their adventure, counting coup. . . .

But she had not gone with them. There was no way she could have remembered that bridge across the creek, the trail going up out of the evening light.

Still, how could she not have recognized the place as a whole—the forest, the cabins? Two weeks of three summers she had lived here, at twelve and thirteen and fourteen, and had she never noticed the silence? the size of the redwoods? the black, appalling, giant stumps?

It was forty years; the trees might have grown a good deal—and now as she thought it did seem that she and Jan had actually climbed one of the stumps one day, to sit and talk, cutting Crafts, probably. But they hadn't thought anything about the stump but that it was climbable, a place to talk in privacy. No sense of what that huge wreck meant, except (like those who had cut the tree) to their own convenience; no notion of what it was in relation to anything else, or where it was, or where they were. They were here. Despairingly homesick the first night, thereafter settled in. At home in the world, as cheekily indifferent to cause and effect as sparrows, as ignorant of death and geography as the redwoods.

She had envied Jan and Dorothy their exploit, knowing them to be a good deal braver than she was. They had agreed to take her back to Boys Camp with them, and hoot and meow, or just hide and watch, but they never got around to it. They all went to Camp Fire and sang lonesome cowboy songs instead. So she had never seen Boys Camp until she came here and sat on the log and watched the poet circle slowly in the pool, and what would she and Jan and Dorothy, fourteen, merciless, have thought of *that?* "Oh, Lord!" she said involuntarily.

The woman beside her in the car laughed, as if in sympathy. "It's such a beautiful place," she said. "It's wonderful to be able to come back. What do you think of the conference?"

"I like the drumming," the novelist replied, after a pause, with fervor. "The drumming is wonderful. I never did that before." Indeed she had found that she wanted to do nothing else. If only there weren't a lecture tonight and they could drum again after dinner, thirty or forty people each with a drum on or between their knees, the rhythm set and led by a couple of drummers who knew what they were doing and kept the easy yet complex beat and pattern going, going, going till there was nothing in consciousness but that and nothing else needed, no words at all.

The lecture was on the Wild Man. That night she woke up in the pitch dark and went out without using her flashlight and pissed beside her cabin, almost noiselessly. She heard no local breaking of wind, but guessed that many of the cabins were still empty; the Men had all gone off upstream, off limits, after the lecture, and now she heard them not chanting but yelling and roaring, a wild noise, but so far away that it didn't make much of a dent on the silence here. Here at Limberlost.

In the low, cold mist of morning, the poet came from cabin to cabin. The novelist heard him coming, chanting and making animal sounds, banging the screen doors of the cabins. He wore a dramatic animal mask, a gray, snarling, hairy snout. "Up! Up! Daybreak! The old wolf's at the door! The wolf, the wolf!" he chanted entering a cabin in a predatory crouch. Sleepy voices protested laughingly. The novelist was already up and dressed and had performed t'ai chi. She had stayed inside the screened cabin instead of going out on its spacious porch, because she was self-conscious, because doing t'ai chi was just too damn much the kind of thing you did here and yet didn't fit at all with what they were doing here and anyhow she was going home today and would damn well do t'ai chi in the broom closet if that's where she felt like doing it.

The poet approached her cabin and paused. "Good morning!" he said politely and incongruously through his staring, hairy muzzle. "Good morning," said the novelist from behind her screens, feeling a surge of snobbish irritation at the silly poet parading his power to wake everybody up, but *she* was up already!—and at the same time yearning to be able to go out and pat the wolf, to call him brave, to play the game he wanted so much to play, or at least to offer him something better than a wet sock on a stick.

Afterword

This story is presented as fiction, but to the best of my knowledge nothing in it is invented except the name of the place, which isn't Limberlost, and the mask the poet wears at the end, which wasn't a wolf. I left out some events and visitors that a journalistic account might have included, but everything in the piece is as exactly truthful as I knew how to make it. The story I wanted to tell was that of a profound gender imbalance in the process of happening.

This was in the summer of 1985, and I was witness, I now know, to one of the beginnings, sources, of what later became "the men's movement." The name of the conference was "The Great Mother," and I was invited to it to read from my novel *Always Coming Home,* which celebrates a society in which gender is not considered to influence ability, nor anatomy destiny. Thus, the quite exclusive preoccupation of the conference leaders with male issues and the male participants was fairly bewildering, and I was the more confused by the double-exposure effect of having been there forty years before at a rigidly sex-segregated summer camp. The only way to describe such a weird experience truthfully, I think, is in fiction.

URSULA K. LE GUIN *has written poetry and fiction all her life. She writes in several modes or "genres," including realistic fiction, science fiction, fantasy, young children's books, books for young adults, screenplays, essays, verbal texts for musicians, and voice texts for performance or recording. As of 1991 she has published over seventy short stories (many collected in three volumes of stories), two collections of essays, three volumes of poetry, and sixteen novels. Among the honors her writing has received are a National Book Award, five Hugos, four Nebulas, the Kafka Award, and a Pushcart Prize. Her most recent books are* Tehanu, *1989, and* Searoad, *1991.*

Her occupations, she says, are writing, reading, housework, and teaching. She is a feminist, a conservationist, and a Western American, passionately involved with West Coast literature, landscape, and life. She lives in Portland, Oregon.

Patriarchy and the Men's Movement: Part of the Problem or Part of the Solution?

Rosemary Radford Ruether

THE 1990S ARE BEING declared the time of the men's movement, a time for American males (primarily straight, white, and affluent) to bond together and affirm themselves as males. The gurus of the men's movement, such as Robert Bly, Robert Moore, and Sam Keen, insist that the men's movement is in no way a "put-down" of feminism, but is indeed a complement to feminism. Yet such claims cannot be accepted by women at face value. We need to examine what these leaders are actually saying and whether their messages to men are authentically and adequately a positive complement to the issues of women's oppression that have been identified by the feminist movement. We also have to ask what are the real effects of this movement. How is it being received and appropriated in the dominant culture, perhaps despite the intentions of its gurus?

Some months ago I saw a brief TV report on the men's movement. The male TV reporters assumed a slightly astonished and sneering tone in this report. But, most telling, was the way they lumped together bits from a speech of Robert Bly, images of males hopping about in a circle to the sound of drums, and male rap artists engaging in vicious verbal violence against women. Clearly in the minds of the makers, as well as the commentators on this documentary, all of these phenomena were in continuity. The rap artist calling women bitches and urging men to slap them around and rape them and Robert Bly urging men to stop being wimps and become "wild men" were a continuum. Is this a misrepresentation or is it perhaps an accurate presentation of how the men's movement will really operate in this society?

Let me begin by saying that I have long believed that "we," i.e., women and men, need a "men's movement," in the sense of men who have come to understand the evils of patriarchy, the injustice that that has done to women, and the way that has distorted all social relations. These are men who are prepared to work in solidarity with women to create a new society liberated from patriarchy.

I know a number of such men and consider them trustworthy allies in the struggle. There is also no question that patriarchy does set up modes of male bonding based on a type of comradery that excludes men from sharing their insecurity and vulnerability. There is a place in the movement to liberate ourselves from patriarchy and for men to learn different ways of relating to other men.

But this does not mean that any movement that proclaims itself "the men's movement" can be presumed to be the men's movement we need—a men's movement that would really be in solidarity with feminism, liberating men from patriarchy. It is not paranoia, but simply well-founded experience that disposes women to suspicion toward men's movements that claim to be healing the wounded male psyche by reaffirming "the masculine." Is there a "masculine" or a "feminine" in this culture that has not itself been the expression of patriarchal power relations? To what extent is such a movement really moving beyond these power relations or simply creating a renewed psychocultural affirmation of patriarchal power relations?

The 1980s in American culture were a time of backlash against feminism in which government, media, and establishment intelligentsia conspired together to turn back the modest gains made by women for women in the job market, health care, reproductive rights, and protection against assault and abuse in the home and in the streets. Basic governmental guidelines that defined discrimination against women in education and employment were dismantled, and a barrage of experts once again urged women to go home and have babies as their only authentic "fulfillment."

The American government has been obsessed with building up military hegemony and achieving as close to absolute invulnerability as possible against all "enemies," both in the Second and in the Third Worlds, that challenge the superiority of our "way of life." The end of the decade saw the collapse of the communist world and its capitulation to the Western capitalist system. The initial challenge of the "end of the Cold War" to the rationale for American militarism was quickly adjusted by refocusing American military power on what had already been its covert adversaries—namely, dissident regimes in the Arab and Third World that threaten American control over the economic resources of the globe.

In the Gulf War, American military machismo reigned supreme, exultantly declaring that it had "kicked" the last remnants of the "Vietnam syndrome" that questioned the righteousness of such interventionism. This triumphant machismo on the government level was both reflected in and supported by renewed racism, sexism, and open hostility to issues of social justice in American society. What can it mean that it is precisely in such a moment that we have a "men's movement"?

It could be, of course, that such a movement arises at this moment precisely as a dissenting response to this reign of white male machismo in government policy and popular culture, calling for a critical awareness of the unjust effects of this machismo on victimized women, racial minorities, the poor, and the abuse of the environment. There are certainly elements of such a critical counterculture around in the socialist, peace, and environmental movements in American society.

While tags from these movements may be employed in the men's movement, what is characteristic of its leaders is their emphasis on (white) male intrapsychic self-affirmation in a way that avoids entirely any social awareness of sexism, heterosexism, racism, and class as social injustice. We are given to understand that males should deal with their masculinity by recreated puberty rites in silvan settings, not by grappling with the economic structures that concentrate the wealth of American society in the hands of a tiny elite, while some 30 percent of society, disproportionately women and children, slip below the poverty level.

The problems of men, we are told, do not lie in the boardrooms of elite male power where these men make the decisions that maintain such unjust concentrations of wealth in their own hands. No, the problems of men lie in childhood, in the family in which the male child was deprived of a father figure and was dominated by a strong mother. The solution to men's problems is to relive this adolescent struggle to free himself from his mother and reclaim the absent father. By reclaiming a strong, masculine psyche, men can heal their wounded masculine identity.

No analysis needs to be made of why the family has been structured in such a way as to leave the primary parenting and domestic labor to women. One does not have to place this family pattern in its larger social context of male public power. The men of the men's movement appear unaware of such encompassing social structures that shape the family. They present themselves as the tragic victims of maternal domination and paternal neglect. Inner therapy for their wounded masculine psyches, not social transformation of the systems that create these distorted patterns, is the solution.

The extraordinariness of such a claim seems to escape us. Let us imagine a parallel "white people's movement" arising that would claim to solve racism primarily by seeing it as a problem of the wounded white psyche. We are told that white people are deeply wounded by the lack of positive white role models, exacerbated by the "vicious" criticism of white people that took place in the civil rights and the antiapartheid movements. It is acknowledged that white people have sometimes been immature and have used their power aggressively, but this is only because they were insecure in their whiteness. What is needed is to restore white people's confidence in whiteness as a manifestation of strong and positive psychic traits.

For too long the white person has sought to integrate the "dark side" of themselves. While this is necessary, it has gone too far, making white people weak and diffident about their whiteness. It is time, therefore, to reclaim whiteness as the embodiment of powerful positive archetypes: the archetypes of Mastery, Wisdom, Goodness, Purity, and Beauty. The therapist presents rituals and journeys by which white people can encounter and reclaim these positive images of masterful, wise, good, pure, and beautiful whiteness.

Journeys to regions of pure white sands and skies are recommended in which white people, dressed in white sheets, can dance around a birch wood fire, brandishing symbols of white power. Blond, milky-skinned girls will present the dancing males with bouquets of white flowers. Would anyone imagine that this is a positive response to racism? Perhaps David Duke might become the cultural hero of such a white men's movement.

Let me reiterate that I believe that patriarchy does distort men's lives, as well as those of women. The struggle against patriarchy cannot be won simply by a women's movement. Patriarchy is itself the original men's movement, and the struggle to overthrow it must be a movement of men as well as women. But men can only be authentically a part of that struggle if they are able to acknowledge the injustice of their own historical privilege as males and to recognize the ongoing ideologies and economic, political, and social structures that keep such privilege in place.

In short, men must begin by acknowledging their public reality as males in patriarchal society, and not retreat to a privatized self that avoids accountability for that public world. They must see that the private self is not an autonomous entity, but a dependent appendage of these social power relations. To the extent that the leading gurus of the men's movement not only fail to do that, but exalt the traumas of socialization of this dependent private self as the only reality, they avoid and deny such accountability.

Worse still, much of the re-presentation of this socialization of the male child in the men's movement simply reduplicates the very patterns by which, again and again, the male in patriarchal society has always moved from the nursery to the playing fields to the killing fields—overthrowing the mother and reclaiming the absent father as the birthright of male domination over women. This is the puberty rite of every patriarchal society; it appears that the American men's movement has not departed from, but is simply reiterating, the old scripts.

ROSEMARY RADFORD RUETHER *is the Georgia Harkness Professor of Applied Theology at the Garrett-Evangelical Theological Seminary and a member of the Graduate Faculty of Northwestern University in Evanston, Illinois. She received her Masters and Doctoral degrees at the Claremont Graduate School in Claremont, California. She is the author or editor of twenty-three books and numerous articles on religion and social justice issues. Her most recent book, published by HarperSanFrancisco in 1992, is* Gaia and God: An Ecofeminist Theology of Earth-healing.

mins movement???
a page drama

hattie gossett

#1: *dear reader*

WELCOME. THE PAGE drama youre about to participate in aims to speak through an ironic satirical character voice to some of the questions raised by the emergence of a mins movement in these days of patripower. the character—*girlfriend*—bombards us with random questions organized under vague subject headings at a relentless pace the better to express herself. you might feel girlfriend is responding to a particular someone/thing. in fact shes practicing "backtalk" an african american oral tradition wherein one actually talks back to the power of the printed page or tv/movie screen or live public speaker or performer.

those whose class or cultural m.o. dictates deep dignified silence in the face of power find backtalk savage ignorant rude annoying quaint. backtalkers sometimes get asked to leave places. this has happened to the author & certain people she knows. once backtalk gets going it has a life of its own. it just runs. so when girlfriend

19

hits her stride shes "runnin it" cuz her backtalk has become its own thing—runnin far past reaction & into action.

now that you know the context our page drama has begun. on the next page please find a 2-part multiple choice *prep quiz* to get your blood boiling & establish a mood. then we get to the heart of things on the following pages with *here we go*.

#2: *prep quiz*

below are 2 quotes. select the name of the his-torical figure who uttered these deathless words. good luck. you may start now.

1. "I will continue to slaughter and destroy, and peoples of the world and the rulers of other lands will recount my deeds. . . . Man's greatest good fortune is to chase and defeat his enemy, seize his total possessions, . . . use the bodies of his women as a nightshirt and support, gazing upon and kissing their rosy breasts, sucking their lips. . . ."

   (a) saddam hussein   (b) napoleon bonaparte
   (c) genghis khan   (d) ivan the terrible
   (e) idi amin

2. "If there hadn't been women, we'd still be squatting in a cave eating raw meat because we made civilization to impress our girlfriends."

   (a) redd foxx   (b) george bernard shaw
   (c) richard pryor   (d) woody allen
   (e) orson welles

#3: *here we go*

what? a mins movement? what you mean a mins movement? aint they still runnin the world? what they need a movement for? what? is this some kind of joke about laxatives or something? basking? oh—

bashing? theyre trying to heal the cruel wounds of mins bashing? wait a minute—did i miss something? do they have to wear breast implants false fingernails get paid less money have no power & get whistled at? do they? huh? huh?

well what do they mean? whatre they going to the woods for then? oh? really? sensitive? does that mean theyre against rape now? when they come back from the woods do they issue statements against child abuse wife battering incest lesbian battering? do they pledge that the next time one of their streetcorner or healthclub buddies is running off at the mouth about how he snatched him some pussy then kicked that bitch in her ass these guys who paid all this money to go to the woods with whats his name will they silently organize a small group to take their brother for a little walk & show him some tongue & penis restraint exercises guaranteed to permanently clear his mind of all thoughts of ripping off pussy or bitches or kicking ass?

no? what you mean not exactly? well whatre they going to the woods for then? is it to get in touch with their homoerotic selves? to discover the queens within? to stop worrying about the size of their dicks? not exactly? what? playing drums? dancing round the fire? camping out? is this some more pseudo tribal stuff? a revised ersatz "heart of darkness" number? a bunch of boys playing games with the cultures of people they dont know how to live next door to?

#4: at home

so they really pay money for this bullshit huh? well after their sessions round the fire do they at least know how to hang up their clothes foodshop cook real food do laundry & dishes clean their own rooms apts. homes offices? do they send their wives daughters mothers to grad school then run the house & work fulltime while homegirls be studyin? will they know how to get up in the middle of the night when the kids cry? how about potty training? will they care for their sick old folks instead of leaving that responsibility to their sisters daughters wives or a nursing home?

will they dress the kids do 3 laundry loads fix breakfast carpool the kids to school work all day carpool the kids from school
to private lessons & play activities supervise homework talk with
the kids iron cook dinner wash dishes go to the p.t.a. meeting put
the kids to bed make lunches for tomorrow? will they be able to do
the kwanza cards & thankyou notes? after the divorce will they pay
alimony & child support on time consistently without having to be
taken to court? will they learn to raise 4 kids on missed childsupport
checks? on welfare? in a shelter? on the street?

#5: *in the world*

will they at least have enough manners not to go all the way to japan
& vomit all over the table then pass out in the middle of a banquet
with the japanese prime minister? will they wear 20 lbs. of makeup
tight skirts hi heels & diet compulsively? will they develop anorexia
& bulimia? will they demand that the pentagon fundraise by doing
bake sales? will they learn to type make coffee operate the copy
machine fill out a fed-ex form answer the phone & take a coherent
written message order lunch or flowers over the phone pick out gifts
for their business associates girlfriends wives? will they join the campaign to make sumptuous housing healthcare & food constitutional
rights? will they still own all the means of production?

will they get paid less? will they have to smile more? will they
learn to cheerfully accept racist homophobic elitist sexist stupid jokes
plus sly feels pinches neck bites sex requests & remarks about pubic
hairs in the coke (beware long dong silver!) as good clean on-the-
job fun & not scream sex harassment? will they stop fucking up the
money by trying to keep all of it for themselves? are they ready to
come clean about mins-on-mins sex abuse harassment incest rape? to
stop fag bashing? to cut out the worldwide race/class/gender pecking
order? will they support equal pay for equal work & fully paid family leave? will all wimmins everywhere be guaranteed the rights to
go to school work drive cars & airplanes own property decide whats
best for their bodies minds lives?

which fashion designer will create the clothing craze that finally liberates mins from bulky unattractive long pants & jackets & puts their legs asses & tits on display all the time? will the smart exec mins of the future wear a stunning neon colored latex lycra ensemble consisting of a short tight jacket that emphasizes the butt & the chest tight bermuda shorts with padded eldridge cleaver pouch to contour the penis color coordinated hose to show off the calves & little pumps to point up the strength of the feet?

#6: sex

in the woods will they learn to pull in their bellies & tighten their buns while walking around in hi heels girdles bright red nail polish & synthetic sable eye lashes? will they wear mini skirts in the dead of winter? will they learn to stop standing around pulling on their dicks? will they overcome their fear of going beyond the penocentric missionary position approach to sex? get ready to get on the bottom? outgrow their pussy envy? does this guy teach them oral sex techniques? do they get daily tutorials in the tantalizing ways tantric yoga can enhance sex?

will they put up no-strings money to back the publication & distribution of wimmins erotica—lesbian & heterosexual? produce some intelligent mins erotica & get rid of this dumb dangerous porn stuff? come out of all their closets? will they love taking it in the ass from wimmins? will they stop using sex & money as control mechanism? will they learn to use condoms & dental dams? will they stop equating the act of conception with shooting live bullets from a gun? will they finally understand that they are not now & never have been & never will be the center of the universe?

#7: & in closing

can they invent a painless mammogram machine discover a cure for the common cold & a.i.d.s. & stop teaching doctors that pregnancy childbirth & menopause are serious problems? are they finally ready to deal with wimmins as full competitors in sports & in the market-place? will wimmins get highpaying jobs as chefs? will rock bands rap groups & governments still be mostly all-mins? can they ever stop playing at being warriors & cowboys who we need to save us? are they finally ready to stop running/ruining the world?

are they ready to knit crochet braid hair & make sweet potato pies & quilts? will they quit fucking around with goldchains bombs guns boomboxes & get interested in clean air & other earth respecting activities? will they stop trying to have all the power all the time all over the world? during this depression will they decrease unemployment & welfare benefits? will they ever support the campaign for dignified & wellpaid full employment? get involved in the campaign to abolish wimmins unpaid labor? learn to listen? get serious about the parts of life that arent about power control money?

do these guys wanna help make the world more better for everybody or do they just wanna whine about how hard it is to be mins in a mins world? if not why not?

#8: quiz answers

1 = c

Scott L. Malcomson, "The Tyrants That Bind," *Village Voice,* 14 January 1992, p. 81.

2 = e

T. M., "Schooling Around," *Esquire,* January 1992, p. 33.

---

hattie gossett
writer/spokenword performance artist. makes words for publica-tion and performance. yip harburg fellow studying libretto writ-ing, musical theater program, new york university, mfa 1993.
publication credits: "presenting sister noblues" firebrand books

1988; also heresies, essence, art forum, outweek, jazz spotlight news, divas on the road journal; also various anthologies. performance credits: wrote/performed theme song lyrics for 1991 feature film "a powerful thang" directed by zeinabu irene davis. work is in repertories of vinie burrows, edwina lee tyler, urban bush women. tours as solo artist and with her jazzroots band to colleges festivals conferences theaters.

A Men's Movement
I Can Trust

Starhawk

 LIKE MOST FEMINISTS of my acquaintance, I've responded to the growth of the men's movement with a mixture of approbation and trepidation. On the one hand, we've noticed for a long time that something is wrong with men, and the prospect of men getting together to fix it themselves is a happy one. On the other hand, our history with men doesn't generate much trust that, left to themselves, they will actually get it right.

Of course, the men's movement is no more a single monolith than is the feminist movement. There are ten, a dozen, fifty different men's movements. Some of them make me break into a cold sweat. Others involve and move the men I most deeply love and respect. How can we tell whom to trust?

Feminists long for men to heal. Those of us whose lives continue to be bound up with men want to see them become whole. We dream of a world full of men who could be passionate lovers, grounded in their own bodies, capable of profound loves and deep sorrows, strong allies of women, sensitive nurturers, fearless defenders of all people's liberation, unbound by stifling conventions yet respectful of their own and others' boundaries, serious without being humorless, stable without being dull, disciplined without being rigid, sweet without being spineless, proud without being insufferably egotistical, fierce without being violent, wild without being, well, assholes. This is what we hope our sons will become, what we wish our fathers had been, what we search for in teachers, what we desire in a lover (assuming we do desire men as lovers) and, frankly, rarely find. At its best, I believe the men's movement also aims for this goal.

Our fear is that the men's movement will do what men have always done, at least since the advent of patriarchy: blame women for their problems and defend their own privileges.

What is wrong with men is that they have been enscorceled, deceived, bamboozled, tricked by a stage magician into looking in all the wrong places. What passes for culture is a shell game, a distraction to keep us from noticing when our pockets are being picked and our dearest treasures looted. The dominant culture is dressed up to look attractive, to make us willing to pay any price to be part of it. But for women, patriarchy is like a razor blade embedded in a chocolate cream. We bite down eagerly, charmed by the heart-shaped box and the shiny wrapper, and then suffer the pain. Our gums are bleeding, but before the feminist movement nobody ever talked about it. We kept our mouths shut, and if we occasionally noticed a trickle of blood seep out the corner of some sister's lips, we politely looked away so as not to embarrass her. Feminism taught us to say, "Ow! Hey, this hurts, this is wrong—and look, it's not just me, it's you and you and you. Something is wrong with this candy! Let's get rid of the razor, or change the menu."

Rape, incest, sexual harassment, economic inequalities, reproductive rights, violence against women, and all the more subtle ways in which we as women have been systematically discounted became public issues through the dialogue feminism sparked. That in itself was a great victory, but as we well know, the issues are far from being resolved. Violence against women is epidemic. Friends who work in rape crisis centers tell us there has been an upsurge in rapes since the Thomas hearings and the William Kennedy Smith trial. Women and the children we support and care for are more economically threatened than ever before.

At this moment in history, men are arising to say, "Well hey, our candy is subtly poisoned. It's making us sick!" "Bravo!" we shout. "Maybe now you're beginning to get it." But on the other hand, we also want to say, "Well then, guys, quit hogging the damn box. If you don't want the poison, you've got to stop eating the candy." If you want to liberate yourselves from male malaise, you've got to let go of male privilege.

Male privilege is not a hot, sexy topic on the talk shows. Nobody is getting on the *New York Times* best-seller list writing about it these days. Nevertheless, it has not gone away. A men's movement I could trust would be clear about the difference between spiritual malaise and oppression. Oppression is what the slaves suffer; malaise is what happens to the slave owners whose personalities are warped and whose essential humanity is necessarily undermined by their position. Malaise and oppression are both painful, but they are not comparable. And the necessary first step in the cure for what ails the slave owner is to free the slaves.

If men want to be liberated, they must be willing to let go of the institutionalized advantage they have in every arena of society. Sometimes this advantage is clear to behold—higher pay for the same work, for example. Sometimes it is more subtle: the way in which most men feel comfortable speaking out in a group, while women tend to remain silent and listen; the use of "he" as a universal term; the predominance of men in pulpits and podiums everywhere. Yes, we may sound like nags, pointing out the same injustices we've been harping on for twenty years, but hey, guys, how much has changed?

Men have to listen to women. Granted, we cannot describe for them the subtle flavors of their particular poisons, as other men can, but only women can tell them about the razor. We're still bleeding, over here, guys. I become alarmed when I hear statements that imply that men have already listened to women too much, been made "soft" by the feminist movement. Believe me, there may be three men in the country that have been overly influenced by the feminist movement. Oh, maybe five. Maybe as many as ten. Perhaps these men are indeed too "soft," as Robert Bly implies, perhaps they do "lack energy" (Bly, pp. 1–5), although I can't help but suspect that Bly has simply invented a new term for the old male taunt, "Can't get it up," or possibly, "Faggot." A lot of men I know have been influenced by the feminist movement—for the better, I say, and certainly not overly so. A lot of men are strong allies, good friends, staunch comrades in the struggle. They are not the problem. The problem is the legions of men who haven't even begun to get it yet, who still have to prove their masculinity by ordering bombing raids or humiliating their female co-workers, the men who make us afraid to walk down lonely streets at night. The men's movement I could trust would figure out how to reach those men. Certainly it seems premature to be talking about going beyond the feminist movement when men are still making more money, controlling the government, the media, and the corporations, raping and battering and murdering at alarming rates, and are even now taking away our reproductive choices once again.

This is what makes women so mad. I came into the feminist movement in the early seventies when I was quite young, barely twenty, and immediately got mad. I didn't like being mad; I much preferred the previous movement when I was a laid-back hippie earth mother, optimistic, mystical, and calm. But the more I found out about what was really going on, the more I had to look at the slimy underbelly of the beast, the madder I got. Then it wore off, sometime in the late seventies or early eighties, when I spent a lot of time blockading nuclear facilities in company with large numbers of men who were actively struggling to embody feminist principles and processes in organizing. They often fell short, as did a lot of women, but we were in there pitching, so to speak. And I was deeply grateful not to feel angry at men as a class. By nature I have a rather calm and placid temperament and rage takes a lot out of me. And the division of the world into women/good—men/bad seemed another version of the dualism that was rapidly driving us toward nuclear destruction.

The Clarence Thomas hearings brought my rage back. Wham, pow, oh, yes, men still don't listen to women. Yes, some do—the three in here with me watching the hearings on TV and gently restraining me from smashing the set, but as a group, as a class, as a morphogenetic field, they don't. Neither do a lot of women, for that matter. But if men are going to make any real movement, they've got to start. Listen to women, guys. Listen even to our rage. Yes, I know we don't look very attractive with all that blood on our teeth, but if you don't listen, there are things you need to know that you will never find out. Don't take it personally, don't defend yourselves, just once in a while shut up and listen. And while we're on the subject, stay out of the limelight occasionally. Don't always be the first to pronounce on every topic; don't dominate every arena of public discourse. It's not that we want you to be perpetually silent; it's just that we want you occasionally to listen first before you speak. Just listen. And if once in a while we aren't talking about you, if we write a book that focuses on women or make a film that interviews more women than men or have a conversation in which men aren't mentioned, that's okay. It might be a healthy counterbalance to our five thousand–year fixation on men and men's affairs. It doesn't have to threaten you, it doesn't have anything to do with you really. You're big boys; you don't need mama's attention every moment, do you?

That's part of what I mean by being willing to relinquish male privilege. Feminists don't want men to feel guilty—unless of course, they've done something to feel guilty about. Okay, feel guilty if need be for what you do, but never feel guilty for who you are. Some woman gave birth to you, shaped your male body inside her—honor her by taking pride in yourself. But be responsible. Show some solidarity with us.

And, hey, guys, really it's a good deal for you, when you consider what you've been paying for patriarchy. Every mother of sons

knows that the price of male privilege is the body bag, the para-
plegic's wheelchair, the shell-shocked veteran's nightmare. A portion
of each generation of sons are sacrificed to secure the superior status
the surviving males enjoy. The big secret, guys, is not something you
have to steal from under your mother's pillow; the big secret is that
old men will try to kill you before you grow up.

The problem with men is not, as Robert Bly suggests, that the
male initiatory process has broken down. The problem is that it's
working all too well to shape young boys and girls into the type of
men and women required by a society dominated by war. If you
doubt that contemporary American culture is a war culture, consider our federal budget for a moment, or consider how schools
and medical care and social programs are drastically cut while
money is easily found to decimate Iraq. Or take a look at the offer-
ings on television on any given night, and note how many deal with
one sort of war or another, foreign wars, star wars, police wars. Note
the rhetoric of our politicians, left- and right-wing, from the war
on poverty to the war on drugs.

War requires soldiers. Not mythical warriors, independent, self-
sacrificing masters of strategy, not "a warrior in service to a True
King—that is, to a transcendent cause" (Bly, 151)—not inner warriors or archetypal warriors or spiritual warriors, but soldiers:
weaponlike, obedient to their handlers, and unthinkingly, unfeel-
ingly brutal to their victims. War requires hierarchy, in which those
lower on the rungs are not self-acting but obey their superiors even
at the cost of their own lives. The bodies of young men are dispos-
able, especially if they do not come from the dominant races or
classes that have ways of protecting their own. And war requires
women who are passive, who serve as sexual prizes and breeders of
new generations of soldiers. In a wararchy, the bodies of young men
and all women are at the disposal of others, to do with as they will.
We do not own ourselves.

For women, this harsh truth is the razor; for men, the poison
in the candy of civilization. It's what we're not supposed to notice
or acknowledge or speak aloud. It lies at the root of both oppression

and malaise. How can older men be mentors, initiators, of younger men when old men send young men off to kill and die in war after war after war? How can women control our own bodies when the wararchy stands supported by its boots on our faces?

A men's movement I could trust would face the issue of war clearly. It would recognize that the very term *warrior* functions as part of the magician's paraphernalia, distracting our gaze from the brutal realities of modern warfare, covering them in mythic glamour. Perhaps we should retire the term *warrior*, at least until the day comes when all nuclear weapons have been banned worldwide, dismantled, and their component parts disposed of safely, when we fight once again with swords rather than "smart" bombs and infrared and long-range missiles. Not that we don't have plenty of battles to fight, and much need for courage and sacrifice. But let's call ourselves something else, healers, maybe, even simply fighters, lest we idealize what we are struggling against.

I mistrust men when I suspect them of fudging this issue. Robert Bly writes: "The Vietnam veterans would be in better shape today if we had arranged a festival in every small town in the country, in which the veterans had ridden by, and a young woman had thrown them golden apples" (Bly, p. 197). Of course, given the tenor of the times, the young women in question would have been more likely to have aimed those golden apples at the returning soldier's most tender anatomical parts, but that is beside the point. Bly acknowledges that more Vietnam vets have committed suicide since the war ended than died during it, but this is not because of our failure to provide an appropriate ritual; it is because we sent young men out to risk their lives for ends that were not their own, deceived them into thinking they were fighting for values when they were fighting for profits, and gave them unbridled license to kill. Recently it has become fashionable to apologize for the lack of esteem and honor in which the veterans of Vietnam were held, and certainly our country has treated them shamefully. But the lack of parades and celebrations reflected a more realistic response to what our soldiers had actually done over there—the bombing of villages, the dropping of napalm, the massacres of civilians. Compared to the sickening displays of pseudopatriotism after the recent Gulf War, during which our boys bombed fleeing troops who had no escape and buried enemy soldiers alive with bulldozers, our response to the Vietnam war seems remarkably sane. Better we should have rituals of collective shame and mourning, for Vietnam, for the Persian Gulf, for every declared and undeclared war we have financed or fought in or manipulated into being around the globe, rituals where we stand in the road and tear our garments, heap ashes on our heads, and scourge ourselves to say to our returning soldiers, "We are ashamed. We failed in allowing you to be sent there, we betrayed our highest ideals in what was done there, we share your guilt. Never again. Never again!"

I trust the men I know who are clear about war, and I do know many who are, who have refused to take up arms, who have risked their bodies, along with women of commitment and courage, to stop nuclear testing or prevent arms from being shipped. If there is to be a men's movement I could trust, I want to know what it is going to do about war. Because, hey, guys, you could end it tomorrow, by simply refusing to fight in it. The coup in Russia failed because at strategic moments, the men with tanks and guns said, "No, we're not going to do this." The massacre at Tiananmen Square happened not because orders were given, but because they were obeyed. Yes, women are now in the military, although not yet officially in combat, and both women and men were among those who resisted the last war, refusing assignment to the Persian Gulf, but the overwhelming majority of troops worldwide are men. Why don't men rise up and refuse to go to war? How are they conditioned to be good soldiers? How can they undo that conditioning, and redefine manhood so as to further creative, not destructive, power? These are the issues with which a men's movement I could trust would concern itself. And these issues would tie into all the divides that still lie between women and men, into the deep issues of violence and sexual violence that are bred by war. For example, I would trust a men's movement that made rape the most shameful, disgusting, unmanly thing a male human being could do. Some men do feel this way, and perhaps they can reenvision male sexuality, ground it in a body that can come fully alive only when it is no longer an extension of a weapon.

I am part of a loose community that includes both women and men whose spirituality is rooted in our connection with the ancient religions of the Goddess, the cycles of birth, growth, death, and renewal. Our tradition is called many things, paganism, Wicca, Witchcraft—that's another article's worth of explanations—but the point is that we regularly create rituals and celebrations together. Our Goddess has a male side, or you could say, we worship Goddesses and Gods both, not as cosmic role models, but as constellations of inner and outer forces, as doorways into new realms of possibility.

The Gods we worship have many aspects: the "soft" Blue God, youthful, erotic, creative; the Green God of field and forest, twining vine and leafy branch, grain that is cut so that others may feed and new seeds may grow; and the Horned God, the animal, the wild one whose antlers shine in the dark, fevered with rut, Hunter and hunted, who gives himself away, in his own time, so that others may live. The God is "the proud stag who haunts the heart of the deepest forest, that of the self. He is the stallion, swift as thought, whose crescent hooves leave lunar marks even as they strike sparks of solar fire. . . . He is the moonbull, with its crescent horns, its strength, and its hooves that thunder over the earth. . . . Yet he is untamed. He is all that within us that will never be domesticated, that refuses to be compromised, diluted, made safe, molded or tampered with. He is free" (Starhawk, p. 100).

Our tradition provides us with rich imagery of male power that is rooted in the earth and not dependent on force or violence. Nevertheless, the God is always somewhat problematic. When we create our big rituals, we easily find Goddess invocations that everyone loves, but often have trouble coming up with a song or poem to a God that everyone can embrace. The very images that express power for some of us frighten others. Two years ago, when we were planning a Halloween ritual for over a thousand people, this debate became so heated that one of my coven sisters wrote a long letter stating that perhaps we are incapable of invoking the God at all at this time in history.

Finally, I did what we should have done at the beginning: I went outside, sat down beneath a tree, and invoked the God, for myself. What do you want to say to people in this ritual? I asked. Can we invoke you? Is there an image of male power that can be healing to us, now?

This is the essence of what he said to me:

I am not what you expect to see,
I'll never tell you what to be,
Look outside every boundary,
Where there's nothing to hold to, there I'll be.

I'm the word that you can't define,
I'm the color that runs outside the line,
I'm the shiver running up your spine,
Break the pattern, I'll make a new design.

I trust that God. I hope the men's movement finds a new pattern, a healing pattern. I would like to live in a world where women and men could nourish each other with clean, untainted fruits and fresh-baked bread that all of our hands have kneaded together.

References

Bly, Robert. *Iron John: A Book About Men* (Reading, MA: Addison-Wesley, 1990).

Starhawk. *The Spiral Dance: A Rebirth of the Ancient Religion of the Great Goddess* (San Francisco: HarperCollins, 1979, 1989).

STARHAWK *is the author of* The Spiral Dance: A Rebirth of the Ancient Religion of the Great Goddess *(Harper & Row, 1979) and* Dreaming the Dark: Magic, Sex and Politics *(Beacon,*

1982). A feminist and peace activist, she holds an M.A. in Psychology from Antioch West University and teaches at several San Francisco Bay Area colleges. Starhawk travels widely, lecturing and giving workshops. In San Francisco, she works with the Reclaiming Collective, which offers classes, workshops, and public rituals in the Old Religion of the Goddess called Witchcraft. Her third book, Truth or Dare: Encounters with Power, Authority, and Mystery, *was published by Harper & Row in November 1987. Starhawk's first novel,* The Fifth Sacred Thing, *will be published in 1992.*

Cabbages and Kings

Barbara Kingsolver

I MAKE A HABIT of noticing the symbols on rest room doors, because I believe they are cultural icons. Not long ago in a restaurant I noted that the "Men's" symbol was the routine international stick figure: one head, two arms, two legs, the sort of thing that could be beamed into deep space to show alien life forms what we look like here on earth. The "Women's," on the other hand, showed a silhouette of someone wearing a beehive hairdo and applying lipstick. I observed: These things are not equivalent.

My daughter often brings home work sheets from preschool that remind me how we all acquire this habit of looking for matches. Draw a circle around the things that go together. Salt and pepper. Cup and saucer. Left and right. Romeo and Juliet. His and Hers. When I try to understand the collection of ideas and goals that has come to be called the men's movement, what disturbs me is that it generally stands as an "other half" to the women's movement, and in my mind it doesn't belong there. It is not an equivalent. Women are fighting for their lives, and men are looking for some peace of mind.

I do believe that men face some cultural problems that come to them solely on the basis of gender: They are so strictly trained to be providers that many other areas of their lives are neither cultivated nor validated. They usually have to grow up without the benefit of close bonding with a same-sex parent. They struggle with guilt and doubts associated with a history of privilege.

Women struggle with the fact that they are statistically likely to be impoverished, worked to the bone, and raped.

If there is kindness in us, we will not belittle another's pain, regardless of its size. When a friend calls me to moan that she's just gotten a terrible haircut, I'll give her some sympathy. But I will give her a lot more if she calls to say she's gotten ovarian cancer. Let's keep some perspective. The men's movement and the women's movement aren't salt and pepper; they are hangnail and hand grenade.

I met a friend for lunch today, in a restaurant I'm fond of for its rest room iconography and other reasons. The co-owners, a gay man and woman, are the parents of a child whose family also includes their gay and lesbian partners. Once when my own daughter asked me if every child needed to have a mom and a dad, I pointed to this family to widen her range. I told her that in a world where people didn't hurt each other for reasons of color or gender, families could look all kinds of different ways, and they could be happy. We're still waiting for that world, obviously, but in the meantime I like the restaurant: The service is friendly and the vegetables are pesticide-free. The bathroom has nothing at all on the door, because there is only one. It serves one customer at a time, fairly and well, regardless of gender.

I had come to the restaurant to meet a friend, and while I waited my mind ran from rest rooms to Iron John, so that when she arrived and sat down I asked abruptly, "What do you think of the men's movement?"

My friend blinked a couple of times and said, "I think it's a case of people thinking that feminism is only for women, and if there's a 'Hers' there has to be a 'His,' too."

That's it, exactly. The tragedy is that the formation of a men's movement to "respond" to feminism creates antipathy in place of co-operation. The women's movement is called by that name because women are its heartiest proponents—of necessity, because of lives on the line—but what it asks is simply for all humans to be treated fairly and well, regardless of gender. If its goals could be met, those of the men's movement would be moot points: When women and men are partners in the workplace and the home, sons will be nurtured by fathers; the burden of breadwinning will be shared; the burdens of privilege, if there are any, will surely be erased when power comes up as evenly as grass.

To reach this place, we don't need a "His" and "Hers." What we need is for both sides, the beehive hairdos and the creatures of planet earth, to claim the goal of equal rights as "Ours."

BARBARA KINGSOLVER *is the author of* Animal Dreams, The Bean Trees, Homeland and Other Stories, *and a book of poetry,* Another America.

What Do Men Really Want? The Men's Movement, Partnership, and Domination

Riane Eisler

OVER THE PAST years because of the new book[1] I am writing and my own personal interest, I have spoken to many men about the men's movement, what they think of it, and what they want from it. Some didn't want anything to do with it, dismissing it, sometimes quite irritably, as a silly fad. Others were very serious and excited about their search for new ways of defining what it means to be a man, in some cases pointedly rejecting the stereotypical equation of manliness with domination and violence. Still others were interested in learning to have closer relations with other men, exploring ancient male myths and archetypes, or just using men's movement get-togethers the same way they use Kiwanis and other all-male groups, to make contacts and generally further their professional opportunities and careers.

So, not surprisingly, what the media has dubbed the men's movement actually consists of different kinds of men with a number of different, sometimes conflicting, goals. I say not surprisingly, because this certainly is not the first time the mass media have dealt simplistically with an important social movement, or made it seem ridiculous, dangerous, or both. A case in point is how feminism was associated with bra burning, when in fact in all the years of the women's movement, there were probably no more than a handful of occasions when underwear was mentioned, much less burned. In the same way, the most pervasive media image of the men's movement is of half-naked middle-aged men romping in the woods, when in fact there is a lot more going on in the men's movement— some of it of the most profound importance for all of us, both women and men.

For even though this is not how we have been taught to think of it, the fact remains that women and men are the two halves of humanity. So the social definitions of masculinity and femininity (which both the men's movement and the women's movement are today reexamining) not only affect but are indeed central to all aspects of our lives.

Men in Search of New Identity

For almost two decades, I have studied the relation between gender roles and social organization, both across many cultures and over long spans of time. What I found is that we can cut through a great deal of variability and confusion if we look at the roles of men and women in terms of two basic kinds of gender scripts, appropriate for two very different types of social organization. In one (the dominator model), the domination of one-half of humanity over the other provides the foundation for a system of interpersonal and international relations where one person or nation dominates and the other submits. In the other (the partnership model), linking rather than ranking is paramount and so-called feminine values (such as nonviolence and nurturance), rather than values stereotypically labeled masculine (such as aggression and conquest), guide political, economic, and environmental policy. In *The Chalice and the Blade: Our History, Our Future*[2] I describe these two types of social organization in some depth, tracing their development from prehistoric times to today, and showing how much that is happening in our time reflects the point counterpoint between an unprecedentedly powerful partnership thrust and an often violent dominator resistance.

Here I want to briefly look at the men's movement from the perspective of these two different ways of living and loving. This is not, of course, the first time women and men have reexamined and tried to leave behind dominator gender stereotypes and relations. It is, however, the first time that women in such great numbers have rejected their stereotypical roles of passive femininity. And it certainly is the first time that so many men have joined women in search of gender scripts appropriate for a partnership rather than dominator world—which is how the men's movement was launched.

It has been my good fortune to live with one of these men, my husband and partner David Loye, and to see how his work, too, has increasingly focused on gender (first in *The Partnership Way*, which we wrote together, and now in the book he is completing on the relationship between social structure, gender, and what he calls dominator or partnership moral sensitivity). Another man whose work I greatly admire is John Stoltenberg, whose book *Refusing to Be a Man*[3] is unprecedented in its outright rejection of dominator masculinity—as is the fact that a book with such a title got published at all.

I have also had the good fortune through my work to meet some of the men who have pioneered one of the most important developments in the men's movement: men's studies. Inspired by the women's movement and by the spectacular growth of women's studies courses and feminist research during the last two decades, its aim, as Harry Brod writes in *The Making of Masculinities: The New Men's Studies*, is nothing less than a fundamental "deconstruction and reconstruction of masculinity."[4]

Thus, in one of the essays in Brod's book, Michael Messner calls for a whole new definition of success for men, one that will "humanize" men through a more equal involvement in parenting, which will not only give more satisfaction to men's lives but have far-reaching effects on society.[5] Supporting both these positions is another man I have had the pleasure of meeting, University of California sociologist Scott Coltrane. He reports that his research on couples where men actively participate in parenting shows that this improved and enriched not only their relationship with their children, but also with their wives. And he further reports that societies in which there is high paternal involvement in child rearing are "characterized by egalitarian beliefs and generally similar gender roles" as well as by relative nonviolence in all areas of life.[6]

Other men, such as Mark Gerzon, the author of *A Choice of Heroes: The Changing Face of American Manhood;* James Dittes, who wrote *The Male Predicament;* and Michael McGill in *Male Intimacy* likewise propose new ways of defining "masculinity" that are more stereotypically "feminine." For instance, McGill probes the reasons "men aren't more loving and why they need to be." He concludes that, rather than having "more power and control by withholding themselves from relationships," men's fear of intimacy limits their ability to act powerfully in relations—and that men need to learn that masculinity and intimacy are not inimical.[7]

Men's difficulties in forming intimate relations, and how traditional stereotypes of masculinity inhibit, and all too often cripple, men's capacity for caring as well as for sexual pleasure, is also the subject of many articles. For example, Don Sabo's "The Myth of the Sexual Athlete" is a remarkable exposé of how for many athletes sex becomes a depersonalized, basically callous act. Writing for the new magazine *Changing Men,* Sabo recalls how in the "jock" sports culture he grew up in there was "a hypermasculine" script for manhood that made dating a sport and sexual relationships games in which winners and losers vied for domination—in his words, a "man-as-hunter/woman-as-prey" approach to sexual relationships.[8]

As the psychologist Silvan Tompkins points out, these kinds of sexual relations are integral to a "macho script" of tough, unfeeling masculinity—the kind of script required to maintain dominator-dominated relations, not only between men and women but also between men and men.[9]

This is why the contemporary questioning of stereotypical or macho "masculinity" is so important. And it is also why it is so important for more men, and women, to find out about these kinds of writings (which, unfortunately, are still not given much media coverage), as well as about organizations such as Men Against Rape, Men Against Domestic Violence, Men to Stop Battering, and the National Organization for Men Against Sexism, organizations that offer men a real opportunity to work together not only for fundamental changes in man-man and woman-man relations, but in society as a whole.

The Many Faces of the Men's Movement

This all takes me back to where I started, that there are within the men's movement different factions. Those men who are working for gender equity, to stop male violence against women, and to change their own thinking and behavior so they can work in equal partnership with women, are clearly on the partnership side of the line. Clearly on the other side of the line are those men (actually, only a small minority within the men's movement but unfortunately a larger group outside the movement) openly working against equality for women, either denying there is inequality or claiming women should be, and even want to be, dominated by men. Where it gets less simple is in groups such as Robert Bly's "Wild Man" workshops and other (often also Jungian) groups that still urge men to identify with dominator archetypes such as the warrior and king, while at the same time often talking about equal partnership between women and men and a more generally just and equitable society.

Certainly the impulse behind many of the groups where men meet in sweat lodges, drum in the woods, and tell stories about warriors and kings is the impulse toward a less limited "masculinity." This is particularly true for the white-collar and professional men who can afford these workshops, looking for a new masculine script where men are not so constrained by stiff codes of basically adversarial interaction with other men, and where, as leaders of these groups put it, men can "bond."

But although it is touted as new, the script for men offered by some of these groups is actually not all that different from the old macho script—except that now it's dressed up in New Age clothes. As in the old macho all-male peer groups, once again in accordance with dominator requirements male identity is defined in negative terms, as *not* being like a woman. As in the old macho script of contempt for the "feminine," Bly berates his followers for being "too soft" or "feminine"—and thus "unmanly."[10] Even beyond this, he expresses true horror of being "controlled" by women, from whom, according to Bly's and the old macho script, men must at all costs be "independent." To this end, men must even (and in Bly's script particularly) distance themselves from their own mothers, lest, in Bly's words, they be controlled and contaminated by "too much feminine energy."[11] And, as in the old macho script, power (along with freedom and equality) is still seen as an exclusively male prerogative, and men are again encouraged to bond around male power over women.

One of the saddest things about Bly is that he originally preached that men should embrace their "feminine principle"—that, as he said in the Great Mother conferences he conducted in the 1970s, this is essential for world peace. But of course the contemporary struggle between the dominator and partnership models is not only between different groups; it also takes place within the same organization—and within the same individual.

Still, I cannot help think men like Bly would think and act very differently if all of us were taught a history that tells us about gender relations. For then we would all be familiar with the hypermasculinity revival of the nineteenth century, when, also in reaction to feminism, men wrote of the "horror" of a man, and a nation, losing "its manhood"; defined manhood in ways that, as the cultural historian Theodore Roszak writes, "cheapen compassion and tenderness" and "ennoble violence and suffering";[12] and in the end created the "macho" cultural climate that eventually led to the bloodbath of World War I.

Moreover, if we were taught psychology from a gender perspective, we would all also be aware that one of the ways this kind of "masculinity" is maintained is through the long-accepted, and totally arbitrary, notion (as Joseph Pleck writes in critiquing it), that for a man to develop "normally" he must learn not to identify with his mother—in other words, that the mark of masculinity is a man's separation from, and rejection of, any "feminine" identity.[13] For we would then be aware, as another psychologist, Knoll Evans, points out, that the prohibition against identifying and thus empathizing with his mother is a way of teaching a man not to feel "soft" or "feminine" emotions, and thus not to empathize with any woman[14]—not even, in Roszak's words, the "woman most desperately in need of liberation," the "woman every man has locked up in the dungeons of his own psyche."[15] And we would further know that it is precisely in those societies and families where women are most rigidly dominated by men that mothers are the most controlling of their sons—the only male on whom they can consciously or unconsciously vent their pent-up anger and frustration.[16]

In short, we would know that to the extent that men's groups today buy into the old macho scripts, they are reinforcing precisely the kind of society and family where men and women (and this obviously includes mothers and sons) both consciously and unconsciously hurt one another in all the ways that men and women complain that they have been hurt. We would know that myths such as Freud's Oedipus complex—which sets up the angry sons to take over from the equally angry fathers and in the process "possess" as many women as possible (including in fantasy even their own mothers)—and Jungian-style archetypes that still idealize "heroic" male violence do not reflect the human psyche, but rather the dominator male psyche—the same psyche that today threatens all life on this planet.

And we would immediately see the difference between, on the one hand, encouraging men to feel self-pity and continuing to blame women for their problems and, on the other, helping men to feel empathy for both women and men—including themselves. Finally, we would recognize that men, like women, need and want close loving bonds with *both* women and men, including *both* mothers and fathers.

The Men's, Women's, and Partnership Movements

To me, one of the most encouraging developments of our time is that so many of us are beginning to recognize that women and men share essentially the same needs and goals. Indeed, seeing how through most of recorded history not only heterosexual, but also homosexual, relations have been modeled on dominator-dominated rankings, it is truly remarkable that today women and men all over the United States are working to change these kinds of relations (not only in groups but in their day-to-day lives) in ways that only a generation ago would have been impossible.

That this is not an easy process, I can attest from my own personal experience. But what I can also attest is that it is tremendously exciting and rewarding.

As David and I have struggled with traditional stereotypes of masculinity and femininity, and sometimes with each other, we have learned enormously about each other, about ourselves, and about human relations. We have both developed our own creative potentials in ways we could not have in the straitjackets of the old roles— where I as the woman would have had to be David's muse rather than, as in our relationship, both of us being creative and both of us being muses, mutually supporting and encouraging each others' creativity.

As we continued to probe how gender roles and relations affect such "big issues" as economics, politics, and the environment, we have also come to clearly see that there are ways of changing our insanely imbalanced global priorities. We can move from a trillion-dollar annual global expenditure for weapons to dominate and destroy to the urgently needed (and much less costly) funding of programs to clean up our environment and care for people's basic needs—but only as we leave behind dominator gender roles and relations.

What we began to see is that some of the major obstacles to the more rational and humane social priorities men and women everywhere so desperately want and need in fact are rooted in these gender roles and relations. Take the case of how, in accordance with dominator gender scripts, caring and cleaning work continues to be relegated to women for little pay in the workplace (as in the professions of nursing and housekeeping), and for no pay in the home. As long as this continues, and both women and men are also still taught to glorify "heroic" fighting and killing as the essence of "true masculinity," we can continue to expect that "masculine" activities will be more highly valued and given economic precedence over anything stereotypically labeled "feminine." In the same way, as long as women are still everywhere systematically excluded from economic and political decision making (with the occasional woman who violates this dominator rule generally forced to prove every inch of the way that she is not too "feminine," in other words, that she will wield power in the stereotypically "masculine" way), we cannot realistically speak of real democracy—much less of a really kinder and gentler society.

This is why both David and I are so committed to the women's and men's movement in their efforts to change stereotypical gender roles and relations as part of a larger movement to complete the shift from a dominator to a partnership society. And it is also why for the past five years we have put so much of our energy, and our lives, into helping to nurture and support a growing partnership movement consciously dedicated to accelerating this shift in all areas of life, from the bedroom to the boardroom.

By this I do not mean to say that we think the partnership movement should replace the women's and men's movements. In fact, I am convinced that, particularly for women who have been so long conditioned to defer to and please men, separate women's and men's groups are essential. But we do think that the partnership movement is a logical melding of the women's and men's movements, one that offers a much-needed home for those women and men who are beginning to come together to share insights and experiences and, most important, to work together for personal, social, economic, and political change.

One thing I have learned, first through the women's movement and then through the partnership movement, is that there are traits stereotypically labeled masculine that are in fact excellent human traits for both women and men. These are traits that both women and men can (and if permitted, do) share: for example, assertiveness or the capacity to say what one wants rather than feeling one has to manipulate or placate, as powerless or dominated people are taught they must do. And, as many men are today also learning through both the men's and partnership movements, there are traits stereotypically labeled feminine, such as empathy and nurturance, that men, too, can find and, if permitted, do share—and above all, that these traits *do not* make a human being less of a man, but rather more so.

So for me and for David what the women's, men's, and partnership movements are all about is exploring new frontiers of what is possible for both women and men and together creating for ourselves and for our children and grandchildren personal and social scripts appropriate for a partnership rather than a dominator world. We know that for those of us working for fundamental social change there are still many obstacles to overcome. But we are sustained by the knowledge that if we are successful we will truly humanize society—and thus finally attain what both women and men so desperately want and need.

Notes

1. Portions of this article are adapted from my new book on sexuality, spirituality, and society, to be published by HarperCollins in 1993.
2. *The Chalice and the Blade* (San Francisco: Harper & Row, 1987).
3. John Stolenberg, *Refusing to Be a Man* (New York: Meridian, 1990).
4. *The Making of Masculinities: The New Men's Studies,* Harry Brod, ed. (Boston: Allen & Unwin, 1987), p. 1.

5. Brod, p. 209.
6. Scott Coltrane, "Father-Child Relationships and the Status of Women: A Cross-Cultural Study," *American Journal of Sociology,* Vol. 93, No. 5, March 1988, pp. 1060–95.
7. Michael E. McGill, *The McGill Report on Male Intimacy* (New York: Harper & Row, 1985), p. xvii, p. 255.
8. Sabo, p. 38.
9. Silvan Tompkins, *Script Theory: Working Paper for Meeting of Society for Personology,* June 1984.
10. Bly quoted in Susan Faludi, *Backlash: The Undeclared War Against American Women* (New York: Crown, 1991), p. 306.
11. Robert Bly, "The Need for Male Initiation," in *To Be a Man,* Keith Thompson, ed. (Los Angeles: Tarcher Books, 1991), pp. 38–42.
12. Theodore Roszak, "The Hard and the Soft: The Force of Femininity in Modern Times," in *Masculine/Feminine,* Betty and Theodore Roszak, eds. (New York: Harper Colophon, 1969).
13. Joseph Pleck in Harry Brod's book.
14. Knoll Evans, private communication and work in process.
15. Roszak, p. 101.
16. David Winter, *The Power Motive* (New York: The Free Press, 1973); communication with Knoll, communication with psychiatrist who lived and worked with women in Saudi Arabia.

RIANE EISLER *is the author of international best-seller,* The Chalice and the Blade: Our History, Our Future *(Harper & Row, 1987), hailed by Ashley Montagu as "the most important book since Darwin's* Origin of Species*;" and coauthor with social psychologist David Loye of* The Partnership Way: New Tools for Living and Learning. *She is cofounder of the Center for Partnership Studies, has taught at UCLA and Immaculate Heart College, and has published many books and articles, including* The Equal Rights Handbook, *and contributed to* The World Encyclopedia of Peace, The Human Rights Quarterly, Behavioral Science, *and* Futures.

Will the Real Men's Movement Please Stand Up?

Margo Adair

The "Real Man's" Revival:
Under the Tent and Wild in the Woods

OPPOSITION TO domination is at the heart of feminism. If Robert Bly's *Iron John* represents the philosophy of the "men's movement," anyone committed to social and ecological justice has reason to be extremely apprehensive. *Iron John* is steeped in hierarchical/militaristic thinking. As an ecofeminist, I agree with Bly that industrialism, with its alienation from nature, is at the root of much contemporary malaise. To welcome a return of the kings, queens, knights, and princesses of the Middle Ages hardly evokes images of egalitarian relationships. Movement, by definition, is the ushering in of social change. This "men's movement" is not about social change. It is a backlash—men clamoring to reestablish the moral authority of the patriarchs.

The stand of the *real* men's movement is profeminist, gay affirmative, and enhancing to men's lives. These are the unifying principles of the National Organization of Men Against Sexism (NOMAS). This organization has been holding annual Men and Masculinity conferences since 1975. It is alarming that the "men's movement" that gets mass media attention is what the men in NOMAS call the "mythopoetic movement." The media now depicts this "movement," with Robert Bly as its most well-known proponent, as the sum total of the men's movement. This amounts to making invisible what I call the *real* men's movement—real because this movement threatens the status quo whereas the mythopoetic movement maintains it.

The mythopoetic movement is severely deficient in upholding NOMAS's first two principles. While the real movement dismantles the ideology of the "Real Man," the mythopoets are busy resurrecting it. This ideology teaches boys not to cry, express pain, or for that matter, acknowledge any other difficulty, for these are all signs of weakness. At all times: "Be tough, be strong, fight!" "Grin and bear it." At all costs: "Stay on top of it!" The ideology of the Real Man is an indispensable mentality to implant into agents of social control. To maintain hierarchy takes constant vigilance. Domination depends on an ideology of the protective benevolent warriors on one side and rapists on the other. We live in a world whose social order is kept in place by the notion that men are naturally aggressive and territorial. Men are predators, while women are naturally passive, reserved and vulnerable—open prey for male aggression. Therefore, might must protect the helpless from the rapists.

Controlling or Harmonizing?
One Kills, the Other Heals

I also agree with Bly that it is vital to remove the split between spirit and matter. It is essential to reclaim a sense of the sacred and to restore a healthy spiritual life that includes communion with nature and rites of passage. I am sure that men performing rituals in the woods soothe the alienation caused by the sterility of modern-day life, but to connect with nature from the lookout of the warrior and the "Wild Man" only perpetrates domination.

The concept of "wild" emerges out of the assumption that nature needs to be controlled, otherwise "she" will get out of hand. People who have not been "civilized" don't live under or over nature; they live *with* nature. Indigenous people don't think of nature as wild. In fact, having survived five hundred years of genocide that was justified by the belief that they were "wild savages," many Native Americans take offense at the term. I don't imagine that Indians feel imperialist mentality will be transformed because white men have taken to drumming in the woods. Instead they are likely to feel one more aspect of their way of life is being stolen. *Without the paradigm of control, "wild" would have no meaning.*

Considering nature as wild and needing continual domestication (a euphemism for exploitation) has brought life as we know it to the brink of destruction. For the first time in history, the future of life itself is in question. It is predicted that one-fifth of all species on the planet will be extinct within the next eight years. The web of life is not too far from collapse when 20 percent of its connecting points are broken. It is about time we realize that our efforts to live above nature are killing us, too—living *with* nature is the only path. *Living harmoniously with nature while conceptualizing nature as wild is an impossibility.* Wild evokes images of wreaking havoc oblivious to being embedded in a webwork of ecological and social relations. The image of thousands of men taking guidance from their "inner Wild Man" is frightening.

To heal ourselves and secure the future, it is crucial to remove the schism between civilization and nature. When we cut ourselves, we do not have to tell our skin cells how to mend—healing does not take an act of will. Intrinsic to life is the process of returning to equilibrium whenever it gets disrupted. When any ecosystem gets out of balance, it recovers its balance naturally—that is, if human beings don't block the process. Nature does not need management; when left alone, nature does not go wild, but, instead, natural processes bring about ever evolving states of *equilibrium*.

The purpose of domination is to keep an unequal social order in place—providing privileges to one group at the expense of another. This is not a natural state and can only be kept in place by violence and/or the constant threat of it. Wealth is amassed through a system of exploitation and forced dependency. Those in power take a disproportionate amount of resources and labor, which, in turn, strips the exploited of having sufficient means to provide for themselves. Consequently, their survival depends on those who are the cause of their problems in the first place. This is not what one calls a balanced state. *Without a worldview that justified violence, hierarchy would be in sorry shape.*

If socially sanctioned behaviors were rooted in a paradigm of harmony—assuming people are naturally peaceful—we would not be faced with death and destruction at every turn. We don't need the return of the benevolent warrior to protect the king's property rights whether over land or women. *We need to extricate territorial thinking out of our psyches.*

Culture of Denial: Owners Never Own Up to Their Own Power

No one wants to acknowledge that their comforts are made possible through the suffering of others. It is taboo to name power. In the U.S., money equals power. When was the last time you asked someone how much their salary was or how much they stood to inherit or how large their trust fund was? No one wants to talk about the power he or she *does* have. We each only speak about how we are oppressed or how terrible the conditions are for all those "disadvantaged" people—as if there were no relationship between being disadvantaged and being advantaged. Privilege is access to resources, protected by institutionalized control, backed up by violence. *There can be no progressive social movement without addressing issues of power.*

Nowhere in the pages of *Iron John* is the subject raised. This omission amounts to an evasion of the real issues and therefore the perpetuation of institutionalized power relations. Instead, Bly has a propensity toward painting men as oppressed by women—the absurdity of this position is obvious to anyone who is not being mesmerized by myth and faces the truth that American women live with every day. This reality is reflected in the following facts. Women only make sixty-six cents to every dollar men make, and a man with only a high school diploma makes a thousand dollars a year more than a woman with a four-year college education. The violence that upholds this status quo has reached epidemic proportions: Every eight seconds a man beats a woman—that amounts to nearly five hundred women encountering male brutality every hour! Some 100,000 rapes were reported in 1990. If that is not appalling enough, it is estimated that only one rape in eight is reported; therefore, it is likely that 800,000 women were raped by men in that year! It is no wonder so many men prefer myth to reality.

There is nothing unusual about Bly's approach. When power is taboo to name, then history goes through a metamorphosis. It becomes mythology. The mainstream portrays history through images that protect the virtue of the "American Dream." Columbus is lost, but gets credited for discovering America, no matter that people had been living here for thousands of years. Genocide of Native peoples is reduced to cowboy and Indian movies. Slavery is heroically resolved by the Civil War. The stealing of northern Mexico is called "settling the West." To protect our humanity, Americans have developed a culture of *polished ignoring*, otherwise known as denial. As Americans we have a short memory; our history disappears from view, so our social relationships don't enter our consciousness, and everything is seen as an outgrowth of the successes or failures of individuals.

Missionaries for the Politically Correct

It is deeply ingrained in the psyches of all Americans to think in *individual* terms. Even those of us who know the personal is political typically view failure as our own fault and become arrogant when we succeed. Becoming antiracist for white people has many similarities to becoming antisexist for men. Living and learning immersed in a culture of denial, most white people do not find out what is behind affluence. It is to our credit when we take the time to uncover the truth behind what makes our comforts possible. Upon learning the true history of people of color in the U.S. and the fact that they are more than twice as likely to live in poverty than whites are, we whites usually respond with a deep self-loathing, as though we are *individually* to blame. We feel profoundly guilty. We often lose a sense of our own legitimacy, cave in on ourselves, and become crusaders for the cause—vigilantly on the lookout for any individual who might possibly be construed as a racist. When spotted, we go on a rampage to expose and purge the offender who more often than not, has no idea what specifically s/he did wrong. This is because the cultural norms that uphold white privilege are taken for granted and are therefore invisible to those who have it. It is only through a process of consciousness-raising that anyone in the position of privilege comes to understand how their worldview is racist or sexist. Needless to say, the atmosphere created by the politically correct crusaders does not exactly lend itself to learning, instead the ones who need to learn have left the scene so as to avoid further trashing. What really motivates the PC zealots is their frenzied need to absolve themselves of their own guilt and recover their legitimacy. They do this by proving to themselves, and the rest of the world, that they are different from their peers. This pattern of righteousness, the politically correct syndrome, created an open invitation on which the right wing capitalized. This syndrome has driven many allies into reaction.

Guilt convolutes individuals and makes progressive change impossible. It is rooted in individualist thinking, which in turn, is kept in place by having no historical perspective. Not only has the history of people of color been distorted, white people have also been denied their history. For example, nearly every American knows the song "Amazing Grace," yet most of us are unaware it was written by a man named John Newton, the captain of a slave ship who became a leading abolitionist. We don't learn about our foremothers and forefathers who refused to strike the deal—relinquish loyalty to principle in exchange for getting onto the ladder of upward mobility. (Challenging the rules has never been the way to get, much less keep, a job. And if promotion is what is strived for, then learn the rules and enforce them on those a rung below.) Not all people of European descent have colluded with the racist policies in this country. When we learn of our antiracist predecessors, we are freed from guilt, can take pride in our heritage, and can work for social justice out of a position of integrity.

It is imperative that we reclaim our history. Up until recently men who took a principled stand in relation to women's rights were also hidden from us. I applaud Kimmel and Mosmiller, who have just published *Against the Tide: Pro-Feminist Men in the United States 1776–1990* (Beacon). It took them five years to uncover this unprecedented five hundred–page documentary history. This work empowers men to move beyond guilt. (When men have a heritage they can take pride in, they won't have the problem Bly calls "going soft.")

In addition to feeding the hunger for a spirituality, the mythopoetic movement is popular because it offers a respite from the righteousness of PC crusaders. Men's retreats offer a space to restore their humanity in a context that is not fraught with the potential humiliation of being nailed on their sexism. But ultimately the efforts are futile, for the only way to restore lost humanity is through working to bring about justice. Humanity was lost by capitulating to an unjust system in the first place. The golden key to men's well-being does not need to be stolen out from under their mother's pillow, as Bly tells us; men simply need to join the collective struggle to bring about justice.

Spirituality without an analysis of power is dangerous, but social-change activism without honoring everyone's humanity will lead us nowhere. If, by a fluke, we do get anywhere, it is likely to feel strikingly familiar. We are fully capable of duplicating relations of domination, with no institutional backup, despite our best intentions. We must have a generosity of spirit toward one another as we support each other in the simultaneous struggle to transform ourselves and bring about social justice.

Patterns of Power

Male privilege is only one form of power among many: class privilege, white-skin privilege, heterosexual privilege, to name a few. Power, no matter what kind, is kept in place through the same patterns of domination. These patterns force the privileged to stiffen up: be emotionally suppressed, remote, and alienated so that the inhumanity of controlling others is *not felt*. "Control yourself so you can control others without flinching." (Have you ever noticed that the more privilege people have, the more control patterns they exhibit, and the further away from power, the more spontaneity, humor, and open affection people display?) To oppress others it is necessary to suppress oneself; this is not a condition that is compatible with celebrating life. All agents of control suffer a deep psychic pain, for they have been forced to relinquish their humanity.

As a white middle-class woman who has spent most of my activist energy for the past decade on issues of race and class, I have much affinity with the men who struggle against sexism. I come from many generations of upper middle-class WASPS, a culture that has control patterns down. "Don't express affection or vulnerability." "Always maintain your composure." "Be cool, calm, collected, and correct—be in control." As a kid, I had to go on a trip that lasted at least two weeks before it warranted a good-bye hug.

I imagine that what motivates me to work against racism and classism is much the same as what inspires men to struggle against sexism. For me, getting rid of institutionalized racism and classism is intimately linked with reclaiming my right to be fully alive—a spontaneous, joyful, loving, sensuous, feeling being. The more I shed my socialized patterns of self-control, the more I heal my alienation and access communion with others. The more I let go of "having to keep everything under control," the more I find myself sharing and working collectively. I move out of isolation; I get to relax and trust the process. For me, giving up self-control does not mean becoming wild; on the contrary, it means becoming vulnerable, affectionate, relaxed, respectful, and trusting.

When we let go of our shields, we *feel*, and subsequently become responsible for our own actions. When agents of control focus on the *consequences* of their actions as opposed to some myth about knights and princesses, they resign. In *Iron John*, Bly expresses disdain for the young man at a men's retreat who refused to pick up a sword because it was an instrument of violence. I celebrate such men. When we have swords, we need shields.

Bly has provided an alternative for men to reclaim an emotional life. They have moved to the other end of the continuum of control: "Let it all out, go wild!" Like taking aspirin for pain, they never have to deal with the cause of the pain itself. Released from suppressing the self on the weekend, it is easier to return to control the rest of the time. As a result, they don't flinch when they are confronted with the consequences of their collusion with the exploitation of others. *Like the protective warrior and the rapist, wild and control are also two ends of the same spectrum.* It is time to shift paradigms. There would be no need for the "Wild Man" if men would relinquish the need for control. The "Real Man" could relax if the reality of manhood was simply established biologically, not sociologically.

The Nurturing Nature of the Real Men's Movement

Home is the place of nourishment. Men could stop lamenting the absence of a father if nurturing became socially sanctioned behavior for males. Fathers would not need to be remote. I found it interesting that, in all the writings of profeminist men who are part of the network emerging out of the annual Men and Masculinity conferences, there were no descriptions of what positive masculinity might be. It is not that they are negative about men. *Changing Men*, the magazine endorsed by NOMAS, is filled with positive male role models. But nowhere is there a list of positive masculine traits. As a woman, I feel I have no special claim on the qualities of love, caring, nurturing, gentleness, tenderness, receptivity, etc. I think we would all benefit from giving up the duality of feminine/masculine. I would not miss them if we dropped both words out of our vocabulary. If differentiation is so important, I think our physiological differences are enough to keep each from being mistaken for the other.

I have found that the atmosphere created by men in the anti-sexist men's movement to be qualitatively different than any settings I have been in before. Last fall I was invited to facilitate an alliance building session at the twelfth biannual California Men's Gathering, which was to revolve around the theme of "Confronting Racism." I was pleasantly struck by the open display of affection at the event. In the kindhearted atmosphere of the CMG, everyone was accepted—straight, gay, or bisexual. Throughout the gathering, I had an uncanny sensation; I didn't know what to attribute it to. Then I realized I felt completely safe. Here I was, one of only a half-dozen women, at a camp with hundreds of men. The only thing I can compare it to is the sensation one has right after receiving a massage—you realize how tense you were after the tension is gone. It was a profound and unfamiliar experience to be surrounded by men and feel safe. Only men directly engaged in ridding themselves of sexist conditioning are able to reclaim their humanity and openly express warmth. They shed their armor and share their love of life.

Homophobia, in our culture, is intimately intertwined with sexism. Homophobia makes it taboo to act like a "girl"—a euphemism for unwillingness to engage in aggression. Homophobia keeps men from having deep emotional bonds with one another. War and aggressive sports are the only culturally acceptable arenas where it is possible to bond with one another. Without the fear of being labeled a "sissy," no man would have to prove he was "man enough."

Bly avoids dealing with homosexuality. As we know all too well, there is nothing unusual about this approach either. But it is particularly offensive when Bly is addressing male-to-male relationship, and pulls from Greek myth, in which homosexuality is woven throughout, and yet conveniently doesn't tell his readers about that part. He also omits acknowledgment of homosexuality in the traditional tribes he cites.

In dramatic contrast, NOMAS is gay affirmative. It spawned the Campaign to End Homophobia. I participated in their 1991 national conference, which was held under the banner of building multicultural communities. In my fifteen years of activism, I have never been to a conference that was more vibrant and supportive, and yet sharply naming the problems we face. Not once during the entire conference did I hear people ranking who is more oppressed (a preoccupation that has created untold dissension in the women's movement). In addition to the open display of affection at both of these events, I appreciated how men acknowledged one another's work. This was a breath of fresh air after the competitive atmosphere that reigns in most conferences.

I welcome the real men's movement! At the core of this movement is a reevaluation and redefinition of what it means to be a man. A reevaluation that every man must undertake if we are ever to inhabit a world that is both safe and just. A reevaluation that every man must undertake if he is ever to be free of the perpetual proving that he is "man enough," that he is a "Real Man." Men who have uprooting sexism at the center of their consciousness are creating a new culture where they reclaim their humanity, a culture that has shed competition and militarism, and replaced them with cooperation and a celebration of life.

This movement is teeming with vital activity. I thank the men who help other men stop battering and embark on a road of healing transformation. I thank the men who provide child care at events. I thank the men who go to the frat houses to help stop date rape. I thank the men who march against porn. I thank the men whose songs and poetry create a culture that celebrates one another as gentle-men. I thank the men who create profeminist curricula on men's roles in academia. I thank the men who challenge giving visitation rights to abusive fathers. I thank the men who vigil for women shot in the Montreal Massacre. I thank the men who paralleled the Vietnam Memorial with a huge banner bearing the names of the fifty-one thousand women who died at the hands of American men between 1957 and 1975. I thank the men who circulate the pledge against violence. I thank the men who have organized Brother Peace Day. I thank the men who have become nurturers of men, and women.

I say thank you to the men in the real men's movement!

(The author would like to acknowledge Carolyn Adair, George Franklin, Thomas Mosmiller, Nancy Netherland, Pamela Osgood, and Willow Simmons for the tremendous editorial support they provided in the development of this essay.)

MARGO ADAIR *is the author of* Working Inside Out, *coauthor with Sharon Howell of* The Subjective Side of Politics *and* Breaking Old Patterns, Weaving New Ties: Alliance Building. *Her work has always navigated through the realms of spirituality and politics—each informing the other—each incomplete without the other. She founded Tools for Change to facilitate healing the schism across the lines of gender, race, class, sexual orientation, and age, transforming domination of one another and nature to living in harmony where the sanctity of all life is honored. She has been leading empowerment workshops and providing mediations, facilitation, and consulting services for organizations for over fifteen years. She is on the editorial board of* Groundwork, *a national magazine linking the social justice, peace, and environmental movements. She lives in San Francisco. For more information about her work, contact Tools for Change, 349 Church Street, San Francisco, CA 94114.*

Nicole Hollander

Pumping Iron John

Jane Caputi and
Gordene O. MacKenzie

[Gender] difference exists in every cell of the body.
Robert Bly, *Iron John*[1]

THE JANUARY 20, 1992, issue of *Time* magazine tries
to tell us just what kind of a year it is going to be
for women and men. The headline reads: "Why
Are Men and Women Different?" Right away we notice that
another question is not being asked: *Are* men and women
different? The title itself presumes and enforces sexual difference. A subtitle continues: "It isn't just upbringing. New
studies show they are born that way." A dark-haired boy
and a blond girl (dressed not too subtly in red, white, and
blue) stand together. The backdrop is a brick wall. She is
looking at him, with an expression of grinning indulgence,
one hand placed shyly against his elbow. He uses one of
his hands to raise the cuff of his shirt so that he can flex
his biceps, which he lovingly gazes upon. She is looking at
him; she is touching him. He is oblivious to her; he is

69

touching himself. They both gaze at his small swollen muscle. She is pumping him up with her attention, touch, and gaze. He is pumping himself. They are both pumping iron john. The message couldn't be clearer: The women's movement and contemporary women are up against a (brick) wall. The so-called "Wild Men" of the contemporary "men's movement," who incessantly drum out the message of innate gender difference and, implicitly, inequality between women and men, must be chanting "Ho!"

Robert Bly's *Iron John*, the bible of the men's movement, topped the best-seller lists for much of 1991. In this work, Bly laments the lot of "soft" and "faceless" men who remain under the maiming influence of the mother and/or dominant female lovers. He proclaims that we live in a world bereft of male initiation and that this is a society in which there is "not enough father," leaving men "wounded" and beset with grief. Although we'll expand upon these points later, we must take a moment here to seriously question Bly's credibility as a cultural observer. Doesn't the man go to the movies or watch television—ritual activities in themselves, where stories of boys turning into men and paeans to father power are omnipresent. Many of the most popular films of all time concern some aspect of male initiation, e.g., *Star Wars, Home Alone, Top Gun,* and just about anything by Steven Spielberg, e.g., *Jaws, E.T.* and *Hook.* Television, of course, is a medium notorious for its father fixation, from "Father Knows Best" to "The Cosby Show." With some notable exceptions ("Roseanne"), all too frequently mothers play second banana ("Home Improvement"), or have been disappeared by the story line altogether ("Davis Rules," "Full House"), even though, in reality, there are many more single female parents than male. As a recent headline in the *New York Times* (May 26, 1991) summed up current TV demographics: "Poof! The Mommies Vanish in Sitcomland."

Such trends are highly significant, for the mass media serve as our culture's primary dispensary of myth and ritual. Here, stories are told that transmit and reinforce mainstream values, that tell us how the world works, instruct us as to what is normal or deviant, right or wrong, that form both the individual and the collective psyche. Robert

Bly himself is fully aware of the power of story to affect consciousness. In *Iron John,* he dives deeply into the patriarchal archives, surfacing with a Grimm Brothers' tale ("Iron John"), which he offers as an alchemical parable for modern men. In his view, Iron John, a.k.a. the "Wild Man," is the source of "true masculinity" repressed and denied in modern culture, the figure with whom Bly believes all men must connect in order to transmute from boys to men.

In the fable, Iron John is a wild, extremely hairy man who lives in a state of enchantment in a forbidding forest, beneath a deep lake. The king has him brought back to the castle, where he is kept locked up in an iron cage. The king's son accidentally rolls his golden ball into the cage. To get it back, he agrees to steal the key to the cage from under his mother's pillow, and free Iron John. Dreading punishment, the prince runs away with Iron John, eventually undergoing various ordeals of initiation until, aided by his hairy mentor, he proves his manhood by besting an enemy in battle and marrying a princess, at which point Iron John is freed from his enchantment.

During the past two decades, the contemporary women's movement has questioned and rejected rigid sex and gender stereotypes, creating new myths and definitions of female power, and naming ourselves to be "Wild," that is, undomesticated and outside of the bounds of patriarchy (most vividly, in Mary Daly's *Gyn/Ecology,* 1978).[2] The feminist movement also challenged men to invent new definitions of "masculinity" and to make a qualitative break from a world ordered by a "masculinity" understood to be aggressive, violent, and unemotional. At first some women might be hopeful that the men's movement would concern itself with these sorts of radical changes, but, despite some double-talk to the contrary, the song these wild men are singing is "Return to Gender" (that is, rigid bipolar gender roles). Just as David Duke and his followers responded to the pressures of antiracist movements with the founding of the National Association for the Advancement of White People, much of the activity going on under the rubric of the "men's movement" (composed largely of white middle-class men) is a form of masculinist nationalism, that is, a reconstellation of patriarchal rules and roles and an attempt to consolidate cockocratic[3] power in response to challenges from the women's movement. The "men's movement," as epitomized by Bly's writings, while portending/pretending to be a movement for liberation is actually a manifestation of an authoritarian backlash and joins the political and religious right in reinforcing separatism, hierarchy, contempt for the "other," and invidious distinctions between women and men.

Zeus Juice[4]

In his pursuit of "true masculinity," Bly urges a return not only to hairy fairy tales, but to ancient manly deities, notably the Greek god Zeus. Zeus, as Robert Graves extensively demonstrates, was an incessant rapist, molesting both mortal women and ancient goddesses. Moreover, his reign ushered in an era of blight for women. As Graves notes: ". . . the hitherto intellectually dominant Greek woman degenerated into an unpaid worker and breeder of children wherever Zeus and Apollo were the ruling gods."[5] Bly expediently ignores these factors and instead rhapsodizes over Zeus as the embodiment of: "positive male energy . . . Zeus energy, which encompasses intelligence, robust health, compassionate decisiveness, good will, generous leadership. Zeus energy is male authority accepted for the good of the community."[6] Antipatriarchal women and men would do well to defy Bly, the iron-age guru, exhorting us to give over our power to rapist divinities and self-styled father figures "for our own good."

Bly neatly reverses the real meaning of Zeus' "masculinity" and such doublethinking inversion structures much of the movement. If we understand Zeus not as a rapist, but as a benevolent authority, we can more readily accept elite men as victims, not victimizers. In much of men's movement ideology, men identify themselves as victims: of absent fathers, of a contaminating and encompassing "femininity," and of angry feminists and insubordinate wives and girlfriends.

Some estimates suggest that over a quarter of a million men have participated in "men only" workshops, conferences, and weekend fraternal "adventures." Here, frequently in wilderness settings, they engage in drum beating, screaming, chanting, sweat lodging, dancing, crying, hugging, and playing Big Daddy to one another in a dying world (and no doubt terrorizing whatever indigenous animal life still exists). According to the tenets of the men's movement, it is of paramount importance that younger men overcome their distrust of older men and bond together in son-father dyads to heal their wounds. In Bly's view, men have been deprived of initiation into manhood due to the structuring of industrial society that removed fathers from the home. This absent father syndrome, allegedly, is the source of men's deepest grief. To address this pain and to become truly "masculine," Bly contends that men need a surrogate father figure or "male mother" (not unlike Bly himself).

We would not deny that men, even socially elite men, feel grief and have been victimized. All were at one time boys and, as Kate Millet points out, the rules of patriarchal domination are twofold: Men shall dominate women, and elder men shall dominate younger men.[7] In patriarchy, any group perceived as "weaker" or "other" is stereotyped as "feminine," including women, people of color, and even male children. As such, boyhood in patriarchy is frequently an ignominious state. Boys can be humiliated by their fathers with impunity; they, like girls, are sexually exploited by adults, most frequently by adult males; and they are sent off to war (by governmental father figures) to be maimed and killed. By urging men to heal the wound with their fathers, Bly is urging a truce between elite men, asking younger men to identify with their prior oppressors and unite with the fathers in opposition to women and "others," effectively consolidating patriarchal power.

Bly writes: "As I've participated in men's gatherings since the early 1980s, I've heard one statement over and over from American males, which has been phrased in a hundred different ways: 'There is not enough father.'"[8] This alleged father lack plagues not only individual men, but our entire culture, which, Bly contends, is

Completely Belligerant! [handwritten]

equivalent to men's rights activist? [handwritten, left margin]

desperately hungering for "the King." If so, this is extremely alarming, for a yearning for paternal authority figures smacks not of therapeutic healing, but of fascism. As Gertrude Stein, writing in 1937, warned: "There is too much fathering going on just now and there is no doubt about it fathers are depressing. Everybody nowadays is a father, there is father Mussolini and father Hitler and father Roosevelt and father Stalin . . . and there are ever so many more ready to be one."[9] Again, it seems incredible that Bly can gaze upon a world dominated by father figures—father Bush, father Schwartzkopf, father Turner, father Yeltsin, Jehovah, Allah, God the father, and John Paul Too—and see an *absent* father. Of course, Bly (and other men's movement leaders) would contend that many military and political leaders are not *true* fathers, but "shadow" fathers or "Poisoned Kings." This is tantamount to denying the culpability of the Church for the Inquisition by arguing that those who implemented it were not *true* Christians. Bly's argument is riddled further with doublethink, because the archetypes of and routes to "masculinity" that he explicitly prescribes can lead only to this type of "poisoned" (more accurately *poisoning*) father.

For example, we must question Bly's use of a fairy tale as a source of positive gender roles. Feminists for decades have been pointing out the all too grim meaning of many of these stories for women. As Andrea Dworkin observed, in these tales women are either passive lumps of beauty, hence "good," *or* active and powerful, hence malevolent (and often ugly) witches.[10] In "Iron John," the boy becomes a man by slaying the enemy in battle and marrying a princess, neatly fulfilling patriarchal roles and expectations. The princess, of course, is obsessed with the prince (the original pretty woman who loves too much) and, like a piece of property, is passed from father to husband. There is no challenge to male dominance or traditional gender roles here. Bly overtly denies a desire to reconstitute the patriarchy, yet his glorification of rapist divinities and sexist fairy tales belies that statement. Congruent with this is his recurrent use of *soft* as the primary descriptive of failed "masculinity." All power resides with the fraternity of the *hard* on Captain Bly's

Ship of Snools.[11] When ironclad men shout "Ho," savvy women sigh "ho, ho, hum." Haven't we heard all this before?

Bly's endorsement of sexual inequality also is revealed in his constant admonishment that "even the best intentioned women cannot give [the questing man] what is needed." What is required, it seems, is a kind of psychic semen: "When a father and a son spend long hours together . . . we could say that a substance almost like food passes from the older body to the younger. . . . A physical exchange takes place. . . . The younger body learns at what frequency the masculine body vibrates."[12] This sounds frighteningly like psychic and /or physical incest and evinces both pedophilia and a characteristic patriarchal phenomenon: homophobic homoeroticism. This dynamic easily is recognizable in the patterns of traditional fraternal organizations such as organized sports, college fraternities, the military, and the Catholic clergy. Such brotherhoods vehemently taboo liberating, erotic expression between men, but at the same time profoundly encourage contempt for the female and worship of the male, and engage in all sorts of homophobic/homosexual ritual (e.g., the spanking games of college fraternities, the sexual byplay of football language and gesture, and the sadomasochistic and erotically charged hierarchies of the military and the church). These all-male institutions are the true model for the separatist men's movement and long have functioned as a breeding ground of patriarchal attitudes and values (allowing older men to pass their prejudices on to younger men), and the chief setting for rites of "masculine" initiation (which frequently entail sexual abuse of women and/or younger men). So resistant are these groups to integration of the sexes that one member of the Yale Skull and Bones Society recently threatened that there would be a rash of "date rape" in the "medium-term future" if women insisted upon joining that organization.[13] Such rapism is the true face of the "Zeus energy" that Bly so blithely extols.

It is important to distinguish between the separatism (sometimes temporary) of oppressed groups and the entrenched separatism of many elite patriarchal groups. Simply put, when women and other oppressed groups structure their organizations and life-styles according to separatist principles, it is usually a survival technique, employed because the power elites invariably treat us as inferiors, victimizing us (even to the point of killing us), thwarting our efforts for political change, and, in general, rendering life ugly, snoolish, and boring. When men structure their organizations and life-styles according to separatist principles, it is due to traditional elitist and exclusionary tactics, serving to consolidate male power and to institutionalize fear and loathing of the "Other." As Julia Sugarbaker (Dixie Carter) acidly observed on a 1991 episode of "Designing Women" that lampooned the separatism of the men's movement, such wild men deem women to be the "impure ones" who would "pollute the men's sacred circle."

Separating from the Mother, Or, "I Used to Love Her, But I Had To Kill Her" [14]

Along with that questionable juicy bonding with the father, Bly demands that the son commit psychic matricide. In his words, it is crucial that boys make "a clean break" from the original focus of their love, the mother. It's kill or be killed, as Bly spells it out, for "when women, even women with the best intentions, bring up a boy alone, he may in some way have no male face, or he may have no face at all." [15] Here, Bly clearly aligns himself with the legions of mother haters and mother blamers who have swelled the ranks of "masculine" authority for centuries.

A popular 1991 T-shirt reads: "Shut Up Bitch," and *Iron John* essentially transmits that same command. Bly's call for the radical rupture from the mother signals a greater renunciation and silencing of everything female and "feminine" in order to keep up "masculinity." A November 22, 1991, Oprah Winfrey show dedicated to the men's movement groveled to that movement's prejudices by restricting its audience to males. (Have women ever been so indulged?) Self-avowed men's movement leaders and a "Santa Fe–style" long-haired drumming white man preened on the stage. Engaging in group drumming, they sought to "release the beast" within and encouraged men in the audience to express antipathy and anger to women. One audience member was met with rousing cheers when he stated: "When my TV talks too much, I can mute it. [Unfortunately] I can't do that to my girlfriend." Such are the fantasies of late twentieth-century techno-wild men.

Bly's demand that the boy separate from the mother is by no means unique. This dictum pervades psychoanalytic, social learning, and sociobiological theories, and we see it propagated everywhere in popular culture (from *Psycho* to *Home Alone*). Currently, fearful parents can take an insufficiently "masculine" boy to gender clinics run by "male mothers" such as Richard Green, author of *The Sissy Boy Syndrome*. These clinics force the young boy into conforming to "masculine" norms, inciting him to kill off anything remotely "feminine" or motherlike in himself, often through bizarre behavior modification techniques. "Feminine" behavior, such as playing with dolls, is punished, while "masculine" behavior, such as pulling all the hair off a female doll, is rewarded. One "sissy boy" actually was deemed cured after he beat his mother and sisters with a stick.[16]

Other "male mothers," gender theorists such as Robert Stoller and John Money, have promoted transsexual surgery as a solution to extreme "femininity" in boys. Such a mutilating procedure is accepted and legitimated because it supports the ingrained patriarchal belief that one's genitals and gender identity must line up according to the ironclad rule of "masculine"/male, "feminine"/female. Individuals who do not fulfill cultural stereotypes of sex and gender then become not only targets of violence, but stigmatized as mentally ill. Ironically, all of these father figures protest too much. Each, in his own way, goes to extraordinary lengths to guide (bully) males into "true manhood." As this very state of affairs indicates, "masculinity" is *not* something males are just "born into." Rather, many males have to go through behavior modification, shock treatment, and "born-again" cult type experiences in order to achieve it. Remarkably, some extremely tenacious types succeed in resisting "masculinity" (e.g., the drag queens of Jennie Livingston's 1991 documentary *Paris Is*

Burning) and surgical "solutions," but they then remain cultural out-
casts. Implicit in the labors of male mothers Bly and Green is a hatred
of the "feminine" and an urge to force it into its ordained place—females. Such ideology creates a climate of fear and loathing and le-
gitimates emotional and physical violence against women and the
"feminine," even when the "feminine" is embodied by males.

From Iron to Irony

The many dictionary definitions of *iron* include "inflexible," "unre-
lenting," and "harsh" as well as "weaponry" and "something . . . used
to bind, confine or restrain . . . captivity." Bly intends "Iron John"
to be a transformative metaphor and a model of benevolent, affirming "masculinity." Nevertheless, it actually functions as a perfect
metaphor for the inflexible prison of gender difference that patriarchy requires. Clearly, anatomical sexual difference exists, but having a vulva or a penis does not compel "gender," that is, sex-linked
traits and behaviors. Despite *Time* magazine's magical invocation of
"new studies," the question of whether or not there are innate gender differences is fundamentally a matter of ideology, not "science."

Bly mandates gender difference and eternal opposition between
men and women. Indeed, he celebrates that rigid opposition, re-
coiling in horror from any flexibility or fluidity. In grand ironmon-
ger style, he heaps scorn upon fluidity as a "copper" or conductive
mode of being that reduces men to crippled ghouls: "The more the
man agrees to be copper, the more he becomes neither alive nor
dead, but a third thing, an amorphous, demasculinized, half-alive
psychic conductor."[17] Yet, what is so abhorrent in the notion of
"the third thing," let alone a fourth or a fifth? As Virginia Woolf once
noted, "the two sexes [genders] are quite inadequate, considering
the vastness and variety of the world."[18] The tradition of the Native
American *Berdache*—transgendered individuals, generally males
who live as women—is one example of a "copper" mode of being,
indicating the possibility of movement between what Bly would
have us believe are two fixed spheres. So, too, are the traditions of

Drag Kings and Queens (persons curiously unremarked upon in Bly's discussion of archetypal royalty). Devoted to pumping Iron John, that is, emphasizing and rejoicing in the rigidity of two, polar genders, Bly leads us only further into narrowness, inequality, and enmity.

In *Borderlands/La Frontera*, Gloria Anzaldúa underscores the dire need to break down the dualistic paradigm, the foundation of opposition "between the white race and the colored, between males and females." The real alchemical work for both women and men is not to render ourselves into inflexible iron, but to become, in Anzaldúa's words, "*mestizaje*"—a "third element," divergent, plural, holistic—mocking and rendering irrelevant the bipolar paradigm.[19]

Such mockery and reversal of expectation suggests that one way out of the bonds of gender would be to develop a grounding, not in iron, but in irony. *Irony* is "a state of affairs . . . that is the reverse of what was . . . a result opposite to and as if in mockery of the appropriate result." Perhaps, as that superb ironist Valerie Solanas once suggested, males are really "feminine" and females are really "masculine."[20] Perhaps even more to the reverse of expectation, and Wildly contrary to iron man myth, is that these two categories of gender are themselves historical social constructs that shackle the full range of human expression. "Masculine"/"feminine" are immutable facts only in the world/cage forged by those who would cast all men in the mold of Iron John. Women and men sick of being kept in irons might respond to the men's movement by mocking its revival of hoary archetypes, profoundly unsuitable for a world in which enmity and opposition overwhelm us. In a spirit of Irony, we might create a gender transcendence movement.

Bly bitterly complains about a *lack* of father and the need to summon Iron John as a savior for lost "masculinity." Yet, in truth, our world is plagued by a gross surfeit of father power and we suffer under the sign of Iron John. Like the Yoruban God Ogun, whom he resembles, "the wild man in the woods . . . the Father of Technology . . . the policeman, the military, the one who feeds on war,"[21] Iron John is an archetype of antagonistic masculinity. Contrary to

Bly, Iron John needs not to be summoned *out* of the forest, but guided back into it. He needs to be tucked in for a very long snooze at the bottom of a very deep lake.

Notes

1. Robert Bly, *Iron John: A Book About Men* (Reading, MA: Addison-Wesley, 1990), p. 234.
2. Mary Day, *Gyn/Ecology: The Metaethics of Radical Feminism* (Boston: Beacon Press, 1978).
3. *Cockocratic* is derived from *Cockocracy*, which means "the state of supranational, supernatural erections; the place/time where the air is filled with the crowing of cocks, the joking of jocks, the droning of clones, the sniveling of snookers and snudges, the noisy parades and processions of prickers: pecker order." See Mary Daly with Jane Caputi, *Websters' First New Intergalactic Wickedary of the English Language* (Boston: Beacon Press, 1987), p. 191.
4. "Zeus Juice" was suggested by our very funny friend, Dorothy Johnson.
5. Robert Graves, *The Greek Myths* (2 vols.) (New York: Penguin Books, 1955), Vol. 1, p. 117.
6. Bly, p. 22.
7. Kate Millett, *Sexual Politics* (Garden City, NY: Doubleday, 1970), p. 25.
8. Bly, p. 92.
9. Gertrude Stein, *Everybody's Autobiography* (New York: Vintage, 1937, 1973), p. 133.
10. Andrea Dworkin, *Woman Hating* (New York: E. P. Dutton and Co., 1975), pp. 31–49.
11. *Snool* is a word pirated from ordinary dictionaries by Mary Daly in *Pure Lust: Elemental Feminist Philosophy* (Boston: Beacon Press, 1984), which she redefines to "Name agents of the atrocities of the sadostate" (p. 21). Daly with Caputi further defines *snool* in the *Wickedary* as "normal inhabitant of sadosociety, characterized by sadism and masochism combined; stereotypic hero and/or saint of the sadostate" (p. 227).
12. Bly, p. 93.
13. See Phyllis Theroux, "Man and Animal at Yale," *New York Times,* Sept. 25, 1991, Sec. A, p. 23. See also "Correction," *New York*

Times, Sept. 26, 1991, Sec. A., p. 23.

14. Guns n' Roses, "Used to Love Her," *Live Like a Suicide,* Geffen Records, 1988.

15. Bly, p. 17.

16. Richard Green, *The "Sissy Boy Syndrome" and the Development of Homosexuality* (New Haven: Yale University Press, 1987). See also Richard Green and John Money, eds., *Transsexualism and Sex Reassignment* (Baltimore: The Johns Hopkins University Press, 1969) and Richard Green, *Sexual Identity Conflict in Children and Adults* (New York: Basic Books, 1974).

17. Bly, p. 171.

18. Virginia Woolf, *A Room of One's Own* (New York: Harcourt, Brace and World, 1929, 1957), p. 91.

19. Gloria Anzaldúa, *Borderlands La Frontera: The New Mestiza* (San Francisco: Spinsters/Aunt Lute Book Company, 1987), pp. 79–80.

20. Valerie Solanas, *The Scum Manifesto* (New York: Olympia Press, 1967, 1968), p. 6.

21. Luisah Teish, *Jambalaya: The Natural Woman's Book of Personal Charms and Practical Rituals* (San Francisco: Harper & Row, 1985), pp. 125–26.

JANE CAPUTI *teaches American Studies at the University of New Mexico, Albuquerque. She is the author of* The Age of Sex Crime, *a feminist analysis of the atrocity of serial sex murder, and collaborated with Mary Daly on* Websters' First New Intergalactic Wickedary of the English Language. *Currently, she is writing a book on female power and the nuclear age.*

GORDENE O. MACKENZIE *teaches American Studies at the University of New Mexico. For over ten years, she has worked extensively with the transgenderist and transsexual community nationwide. She is now writing a book, based upon her dissertation,* Somewhere over the Rainbow: Gender Revolution in America.

In Search of the Lunar Male: Contemporary Rituals of Men's Mysteries

Zsuzsanna Emese Budapest

I WOULD LIKE TO stand up for the so-called "soft male." I like him. And I think many women also like him. This is the Lunar Male who has found flexibility. The Lunar Male knows how to wax and wane, how to grow into fullness. Lunar Males are identified with the human species as a whole, therefore women are part of them.

What is so virtuous about being hard? Women are tired of "hard" males; like some perpetual dildo, they go through life's emotional events with an unbendable attitude pretending to believe that is what women want. It is boring! The hard male is part of the Shadow Male. He is the current collective male that hates women and children. He hates that which is alive, changing, wild. Out of his control.

The Lunar male has the power to absorb the Shadow Male into his more flexible male magnetic field. But how? Generations of creative work perhaps. But it will take more than fairy tales, therapy, and abstinence from eating yogurt to turn a Shadow Male–dominated society around into a secure mature masculinity. Goddess help you!

Some men are experimenting with ritual to help them make this transition. This is part of the men's mysteries, which I discovered while studying women's mysteries, both part of the rich Goddess culture of our global ancestors. I have written about men's mysteries since 1975 in my first book *The Holy Book of Women's Mysteries*, under the subtitle "Sacred Sons." I agree that men and women need rituals to make sense of their lives, to ritualize what is important to them, to progress from childhood into adulthood, to create community in which to experience and celebrate their lives.

This was demonstrated to me by my youngest son Gabor's desire to be initiated. He was just fifteen years old, I was on the West Coast, so I sent him a ritual based on what I found out from Jane Harrison, the brilliant English anthropologist and Oxford professor who lived between the two big wars. The ritual was a solo spell that he would put upon himself.

There was a lot of strength in this solo spell, the words were old, the deed was unusual, out of the ordinary, secret. I was not there, nor did he disclose to me too much of what actually happened. He was to wait until the moon was full, then go alone into the woods where the sounds of cars could not be heard. Here he was to light a black candle symbolizing his darkness, his past, his boyhood, and recite these words.

> *Appear, appear, what so thy shape or name*
> *O Mountain Bull, Snake of a hundred heads*
> *Lion of burning flame!*
> *Oh god, O beast, O mystery, Come!*

He was to repeat this three times and wait for a sign from nature. The sign, such as an owl hooting, a bird calling, even frogs or insects, was accepted as a good omen, a sign of the presence of the nature god recognizing/accepting him.

While he was waiting there, breathlessly tuned into the woods all alone, he was afraid. It wasn't the kind of fear he had normally, like when he was mugged at gunpoint in Manhattan for example, or when he was taking a difficult test at school. No. He was listening to his own budding manhood, his own soul, his own initiate community of unseen ancestors. In our modern times, he presented himself in the best "temple" available, the wilderness, as a new Kouretes. A fully grown young male. Instead of a bird or snake, there was a crackling in the woods' floor—footsteps! Footsteps!

Now he was really awed. The footsteps came nearer, but haltingly, not in a steady rhythm. He was only halfway through his invocations to the Great Spirit. So he now called out really loud, hoping to warn whoever was on his way to meet him, and his own voice helped to calm him down. When he finished, the presence was clearly behind him. He turned.

It was a young stag with horns covered with that sexy, mossy hair. The young man and young stag looked at each other in bewilderment, brothers in nature. Gabor's fear dissipated; he wanted to kiss that young stag in relief.

The first half of his initiation was over now. He called up his fears, and his fears manifested; he faced them successfully. Now he was to light his white candle, activating/calling down new guidance from his long line of relatives, most of them witches and herbalists, for at least the past eight hundred years. The young stag just stood around, watching him. Gabor named him Pan.

The second part was a chant, again courtesy of Jane Harrison, who found this ritual in the Minoan strata of the birth cave of Dikte in Crete. It was ritual poetry written by the ancient priesthood of Rhea, left to us on slabs of stone. The hymn celebrates the Kouros (adult male), a sacred child of Rhea, the Goddess of the Milky Way.

What an adult male is supposed to do in the world is never articulated by our culture except to make money, get a job, don't take drugs, get a girl. But nothing about his "mission," his sacred tasks, his moral challenges. I chose the Hymn of Kouretes because in this song the newborn child had to be protected from the older male/father because of a prophecy that the son would depose his father. Cronos the father routinely ate/destroyed his own children. Rhea had to enlist the help of her fully grown male children to hide away the new generation from Cronus, to defend the young. To break the chain of abuse. I thought this was still very true. Generals who send young men to be maimed, the president who bombs civilians in order to win elections, millions of men who abandon their families and never pay child support, fathers who sexually abuse their sons and daughters. I wanted my son to be aware of this mythology and his role in it as a responsible male. So Gabor chanted to his stag Pan. Now he no longer felt alone.

> *Io, Kouros, Most Great! I give the hail! Kronian, Lord of all that is wet and gleaming! Thou art come at the head of thy Daimones [means companions] to Dikte for the year. Oh march and rejoice in the dance and the song! This we make to thee with harps and pipes mingled together and sing as we come to stand at thy well-fenced altar.*

He had a choice to change the words, to make them more modern, but isn't "modern" what we are trying to get away from? So keeping the old chant as is gave the mind a chance to go back in time, and feel for those priests now long gone. The stag, the night, the full moon, the candle—they were just as they have always been. Gabor could feel them.

I told him to bring along some drinks and cakes; he was to feast in the woods. Ancient priests always drank some mind-altering brew, wine, mead, fermented mare's milk, etc. He brought with him a small bottle of good whiskey. He also started to drum on his small hand-held drum, but it frightened the stag Pan away, so he stopped drumming. There was more to the chant. Pan preferred him singing and chanting.

> *For here the shielded nurturers took thee, a child immortal, away from Rhea to protect with the noise of beating feet hid thee away . . . Io Kouros, Most great! I give thee hail! Kronian, Lord of all that is wet and gleaming! Thou art come at the head of thy Daimones to Dikte for a year! O march and rejoice in the dance and song! That we make to thee with harps and pipes mingled together, and sing as we come to thy well-fenced altar.*

The Nurturers? Who are the Nurturers today? Do we have any? The priesthood of Nurturers who hide babies from harm? In this case from the wrath of older males. Where are they when two thousand children get kidnapped every year and simply cannot be found again? The Shadow Male, the murderous male, the consumer of kiddie porn, the john, the drug dealer, he "eats" these young people, he destroys them while using them for his own perversions. Shadow older males often exploit the young ones for profit. Women alone cannot fight them successfully. Rhea still needs help today.

The Nurturers must come back and manifest. What Shadow Men destroy, men's lunar consciousness, loyalty to our species can and will rebuild. Women need their energies to heal themselves, too. The female principle of the universe is no longer the sweet life-giving fountain of hope it used to be when she was well. She is beaten down by centuries of poverty and abuse, she is healing slowly through Goddess spirituality, but the Shadow Woman is out there, also. She is the woman who defends abusive men against other women, the women who cannot make the big step toward self-affirmation. She is the one who makes sure if she gets a little power she is going to hurt a powerless person just as her masters would. She is the secret destroyer. However, most crimes that affect large communities are still committed by the Shadow Male. But there is more to Gabor's chant:

> *And the Horai began to be fruitful, year by year, and Dikte to possess mankind, and all wild living things were held about by Wealth Loving Peace. Io Kouros, most great! I give the hail! Kronian, Lord of all that is wet and gleaming, thou art come at the head of thy Diamones to Dikte for a year. Oh march and rejoice in the dance and the song that we make to thee with harps and pipes mingled together and sing as we come to stand at thy well-fenced altar.*

The Horai are the Triple Goddesses who rule life and death and everything in-between. They gave us the word for the "hours" in our lives. When the hours are fruitful, everything is enriched. Dikte, the Goddess of Peace and Prosperity, possess mankind, what a great idea! No more scarcity! No more war profiting, no more death merchants! No more hunger, or homeless people, or poverty-ridden children dying in the gutter.

The Shadow Male doesn't care about wealth loving peace. He is afraid for the little he has got; he never has enough, of course. He protects his privilege against the have nots. He comes from scarcity and fear. He misses the cold war. He misses the arms race. What the Shadow Male has destroyed, the new ancestors, the new Kouretes, must repair, this is the dream of peace.

The chant goes on.

To us leap for full jars, and leap for fleecy flocks, and leap for fields of fruit and for hives to bring increase! Io Kouros most great!

Here is the ritual "job" of the ancient priest, leaping for blessings. Russian folk dances still have the stag leap, where the male dancer comes out and to the rhythmical applause of the audience "leaps" around the stage, almost flies. In my country, the men have many dances that originated from such rituals. They have a "sword dance" for the protection of the land; they have the "leaping" dance with bells fastened to their ankles. In England, they call them the Morris Dancers. Men have the "Stag Dance," which is a fertility dance. All male energies can be channeled through ritual and social honor into positive acts for wealth loving peace. We no longer have a certified enemy on the outside. The enemy is the Shadow Male. And he dwells within. He can be found in all males; he must be transformed by all males. Or at least enough of them to count.

Finally the chant ends with:

Leap for our cities and leap for our seaborn ships, and leap for young citizens, and for goodly Themis! Io Kronos most great.

Goodly Themis in this song shows men's veneration of the Goddess of Justice. She is the summoner of social instincts, in defense of the human community. Gabor was then to act out this part of the chant, and leap about for all the things he needed to bless. He leapt for good grades, he leapt for a girlfriend, then he did his duty and leapt for the safety of the planet, all animals, and all people.

When he finished his ritual, the stag ran away. He considered himself accepted by the forces in nature, recognized through sending him the stag. He did alter his consciousness and reality, but participating with his right brain in the ritual itself, he also made the historical assumption of responsibility for the protection of new life. He celebrated his young manhood.

I suggest to men that the cry/need for initiation and the company of other initiates can be as close as your nearest woods or wild place. Your ancestors are always there, and they have the time. All-male workshops are important to encourage the new manhood to come out and define themselves. Manhood/respect for males has not been redefined since the sword and the gun.

Workshops should be offered to the young for free. Important studies would include the ancient priesthoods of the Salii, for example, and all their important initiation ceremonies during the month of March, when Roman boys assumed the toga. The cults of Dionysus, Bacchos, Iacchos, Bassareus, Euios, Zagreus, Thyoneus, Braites, Lenaios, Eleutherus, Bromios, Pan, and The Horned One were all active priesthoods with their own set of rules and rituals, colors, and symbols. No male movement writer has published about this rich male spiritual heritage—not a word so far! Is it because a woman discovered it?

In the all-male workshops, too, there ought to be more real ritual, and less therapy. While therapy and its "feel-good games" can be initially helpful in dealing with the father/mother wounds, lost identities, and the dysfunctional emotional lives of men, there is a point beyond which blaming the parents—blaming "demanding" women—must give way to the more adult path of taking responsibility for one's *current* times and the actions of what the collective males allow themselves to do. The Shadow Male must be confronted and healed.

Form your own grassroots men's priesthood with research, then practice the Sacred Dances. Perform blessings and volunteer your time to remedy real modern problems, such as the struggle against abuse of all kinds. Be visible in the political/spiritual arena. Practice ritual and parallel practice activist politics; the two are one, you know. Those who say spirituality is not the highest form of politics have not really practiced ritual. Magical practitioners *know* the political implications of every thought, word, every act, every dance in ritual.

I suggest to the new men to form antirape squads (as women did back in 1972), interfere when you hear a cry for help, male or female. Don't be just a "consumer" of yet another fashionable living room topic, "the men's movement." Make it a real movement; don't let it be just a workshop cult for the few. Reach out to your poorer men's groups. Formulate ideas that can attract the black and yellow and brown and red men as well. Manifest men's centers, where courses are free. Manifest marches against violence, battle the "Shadow Man" openly and tame/absorb him. This is truly your challenge. Your sisters and mothers and lovers depend on your full awakening. We have waited for you so long!

You will experience flack thrown at you as it was thrown at the fledgling women's movement twenty-some-odd years ago: "You are elitists! You are just a small group of rabid radicals! You have no sense of humor!" Let them. My mother used to say, "If you have no enemies, you have not done anything important."

Continue on a spiritually inspired path and you will fulfill your long prophesied destiny, the downfall of the old order, patriarchy. Rhea has spared you and given a stone (her resistance, her liberation) to the old Cronus to eat instead of your tender flesh. Make yourself a talisman, a red magical bag, a green stone for good luck and further growth. Go out under the full moon and say:

Happy am I, on the weary sea
Who has fled the tempest and won heaven.
Happy who so risen free
above his dark striving!
May the Flow be with me!

Welcome Home, Lunar Males!

ZSUZSANNA EMESE BUDAPEST *is the first genetic witch in the USA who put together feminism with witchcraft and sparked/created the Women's Spirituality Movement, otherwise known as the Goddess Movement. Z's first book, published in the early seventies,* The Feminist Book of Lights and Shadows, *received wide readership and later graduated into a larger volume called* The Holy Book of Women's Mysteries. *She led the first feminist coven called the Susan B. Anthony coven Number One, a role model for the country with many more feminist covens to follow. She has the first Goddess TV show, "13th Heaven," on cable TV. Her latest books are* The Grandmother of Time *and* Grandmother Moon, *both by HarperSanFrancisco. Z lives in the San Francisco Bay Area and teaches throughout the world. She has just finished* The Goddess in the Office, *another HarperSanFrancisco release, due out in 1993.*

Essential Lies: A Dystopian Vision of the Mythopoetic Men's Movement

Laura S. Brown

IT SAYS SOMETHING about the ability of patriarchy to confuse women's thinking that I, who can usually sit down at the computer and simply state what is on my mind about almost any topic, have been for the last hour forthing and backing and deleting lines and acting as a well-trained woman in that I cannot seem to find my voice. I have become aware, in this process, of what is stopping me, of my fears of what will happen to me if I say here what I believe to be true. Some attorney for a batterer or rapist or sexually abusive therapist will use it to try to discredit me in court, to prove that I am a radical man-hating dyke whose expert opinions on male violence against women and its mental health consequences should be ignored because of my terrible bias. Because, you know, in patriarchy, any opinions critical of its institutions are prima facie "nonobjective," and "biased"; this is the lesson I have learned as an expert witness in the so-called justice system.

When I realized that my problem with writing was that I was busily trying to find a way to say what I thought without really being clear about it, I shut off the computer and did something to get myself back on track. I went back and reread some of the essays in a book called *Refusing to Be a Man* by John Stoltenberg, a profeminist white male antipornography activist, and reminded myself that if he was willing to be a traitor to his class, then why should I not be loyal to my own and also tell the truth? And I was also reminded— brought back into my mind and my knowing—about how powerful is that most original of men's movements, the movement that is patriarchy, whose intellectual and emotional outposts continue to live on inside my mind. Reminded of why it was, when Kay's letter first came inviting me to participate, that I said yes without thinking even though I have a pile of other writing projects to do. Reminded that I have a lot of things I have been thinking about this men's movement for quite a while now.

How do I feel; I, a lesbian feminist Ashkenazic Jewish woman, a clinical psychologist who works with and testifies for the survivors of violence and exploitation; how do I feel about the mythopoetic men's movement? I feel frightened, and angry, and critical, and amused. I think that anything which is so terrifically attractive to white, middle-class, heterosexual men (for who else is buying *Iron John* in hardback, who else able in these recession times to fork out the dollars for a "men's wisdom retreat") is probably very dangerous to women. I say this knowing that women friends of mine have bought this book for their husbands, and that women colleagues of mine have proposed that our organization of psychologists sponsor Robert Bly to speak under our auspices. But then, again, many women have been drawn to the codependency movement, which I see as one of the most powerfully subtle attempts to pathologize and undermine women's normative ways of being that I've encountered in a long time. I do not think that what is dangerous to women can be calibrated by some women's liking of it.

And I am not surprised at all that this phenomenon has arisen now, in the midst of the Reagan-Bush era, side by side with the rest of the backlash against women and other nondominant groups that Gloria Steinem first identified for us in her brilliant essay "Night

Thoughts of a Media Watcher," and which Susan Faludi has more recently enlarged upon in her book *Backlash*. The zeitgeist has become increasingly overt in its woman-blame in the past decade, and this movement reflects its times. It is not the men's movement of the late 1970s in which I saw some white men take the first few tentative steps toward responsibility for their power. It is a movement for the 1990s, retro like much else that is in fashion.

So let me take each of my reactions and examine them, which is my tendency, being a psychologist and a therapist. Fear first. Why should I be frightened of a group of men getting together to bang on drums and talk about their feelings and awaken the wild man within? What's the threat? If you watch "Murphy Brown" long enough, you might even think it's only pathetic and funny. But it's not a joke. The reasons for my fear are complex, and rooted in my own heritage.

The mythopoetic men's movement defines manhood in a variety of ways that also imply definitions of and attitudes toward women. These definitions are, to begin with, essentialist; that is, they propose that there is a basic, probably biological essence of maleness that is present across time and culture in every human creature with a Y chromosome. It is this maleness that the rituals of the men's movement seeks to honor and evoke, to rescue from the "feminizing" trappings of civilization. The complementary notion is that women can also be defined in such an essential manner, and that there are characteristics and ways of being that are essentially and forever female (claims that have, unfortunately, been made by some feminist thinkers, and that have been extraordinarily popular.)

Leaving aside for a moment my social constructivist intellectual critique of essentialism, with its tendencies toward racism and ahistoricism, I know that at the core I am always frightened by essentialist notions, be they of gender, race, religion, fill-in-the-blank, because of their terrible propensity for feeding fascism. If something is *innately* so about men, or women, then we can be certain that, not long after it has been so defined, someone will be attempting to legislate a certain way of being for us, just in case we've missed our "natural," innate calling. Living in cultures where there are tremendous imbalances of power in favor of men, such legislation is rarely going to be for women's benefit, and often will endanger our souls, our bodies, or both.

For the potential outcomes of such notions, I find myself reviewing some of the dystopian speculative fiction that I have read (all of it, interestingly, written by women). Look at the Gilead of Margaret Atwood's *The Handmaid's Tale*—an essentialist theocracy in which the experiences of men seem to be natural outgrowths of the mythopoetic men's movement, where men raise men, consort with men, and relegate women to their places as caretaker and birthgiver. Or, for a bleaker vision of where the essentialist perspective of this men's movement can lead us, try the books of Suzy McKee Charnas. Her reality, in *Walk to the End of the World* and *Motherlines,* is one in which male children are wrested from their mothers at birth, raised in a postnuclear wasteland to be "heroes" and warriors who do not even know that women are of the same species, imprisoning women as slaves and animals who are underfed, raped, and then beaten for stealing men's maleness during heterosex. These men model themselves on the heros of the Trojan War, looking to myth for their self-definition.

Don't tell me "it can't happen here," that no such terrible outcome can arise from something as apparently silly as men in a room with a drum. As a Jew, I know better; Hitler and his gang began as just a fringe-group joke to the assimilated Jews of Germany. Hitler, too, looked to myth and legend, and to what was "essentially German" to feed his murderous visions of reality; he, too, relied upon ritual, upon the special bonds between men, to build his movement. Millions of Jews and Gypsies and queers died in his attempts to make those myths real, my great-grandfather and my partner's grandparents among them.

Next, anger. Or perhaps, outrage might be a better word for what I feel on this dimension. While individual men may not be any more the knowing beneficiaries of the best of patriarchal privilege than I am, the reality is that they do benefit more than they are willing to admit. Men, in general, especially the white men who populate most of this men's movement, do not fear walking on their own street at night, or being alone in their own homes, because they are not for the most part at risk of violence every day of their lives simply for being male. In every race and class, the men will make more money than the women, and are far less likely to be sexually harassed on the job or disbelieved by their physician, and thus dangerously misdiagnosed when they complain of a chronic pain. The list of privileges that men get just for being male goes on and on. A man who murders his wife is more likely to be convicted of manslaughter, even when, as is most usually the case, the murder is the last act of his battery of her; a woman who kills in self-defense in the same context is more likely to spend the rest of her life in jail convicted of first-degree murder.

So I am angry at the tendency of this men's movement to portray men as the victims, the *real* victims (as versus women? I wonder). Where, I ask, are the John Stoltenbergs, the men willing to stand with women and say that the world will change for men only when men change their treatment of women and give up what he calls "rapist ethics"? Stoltenberg is able to describe many of the same dilemmas faced by men—alienation from self, problems of intimacy—without shirking responsibility for how men have largely created and constructed their own definitions and difficult realities, while attempting to impose those definitions on women as well. Why, I wonder, is it that Stoltenberg's book, which I believe to be one of the most accurate pieces of writing and analysis about men in the English language, is not on the top if the best-seller list; why is he not being lionized by Bill Moyers and paid huge sums to speak to the public? Mary Daly teaches us to look at patriarchal reversals in thinking, and this is a case of such a reversal that angers me. I am angry that this men's movement identifies the problem with men as related to their attachments to women, implying that the failure of father-son relationships is women's doing, and the root of all evil. I am angry that this mythopoetic movement seems to be attempting to rehabilitate patriarchy by dressing it in the garments stolen from a variety of indigenous cultures that have been destroyed or suppressed by the spiritual ancestors of the white men in this movement.

And now for criticism, which is a second-order emotion, mixed with intellect. There are a variety of dimensions on which I find myself critical of this men's movement, but they seem to cluster along the factor of triviality. Women and children are being beaten and raped at home—by men; air and water are growing more toxic by the moment, thanks to industries owned and run—by men; funding for social programs is being cut to the bone by government dominated—by men. And these guys are getting together to lament that they never knew their fathers!?

Now, as a therapist, I know that this is a genuine source of pain for men, and part of me rejoices that some men are beginning to see how they have disowned their pain and acted it out onto the bodies and lives of women, because when they do, we can all get to heal. But my vision of a "movement" is one that calls out for political awareness and activity, that mixes consciousness-raising and the speaking of bitterness with action to change the world. When the reins of change lie in the hands of men, what do I think a men's movement should be doing? Not getting together for sweat lodges and heightened sensitivity to one's own feelings; not unless the sweat lodge is accompanied by action in alliance with the indigenous people whose ritual this is, not unless the newly found ability to cry is coupled with a commitment to learn how to truly listen to the tears of others. While feminism has had many problems, one of them has *not* been an inattention to the need to change the world that is the source of so much of our pain. We talked about rape, then went out to change the laws, build rape crisis centers, teach self-defense classes; when we talked about woman-battering, we founded shelters.

It is interesting that, as I write this, I think of some local groups of African-American men who have come together in Seattle to serve as mentors and role models for their younger cohorts. These men are not bemoaning their fates as African-American males, although well they could; they are more likely to die violently and young, to be hassled by the police just for being there, to suffer endless insults to soul and spirit, than the middle-class white men of the movement. But they are not mourning; they are organizing, acting to change their world, giving to African-American children what is necessary to survive and thrive in racist America. Where, says my critical voice, is this spirit in the mythopoetic men's movement?

I now wonder, as I approach the end of my writing, whether I am truly amused by this phenomenon, or whether my so-called amusement is simply my criticism shaded in slightly friendlier tones. Because when I read my own thoughts clearly on the blinking blue-green screen, I do not find the mythopoetic men's movement funny. As a Jew, I know that my culture has a long history of laughing in the face of the oppressor in order to reduce his power in our souls; if you can find what's funny about the czar, you won't be quite so devastated when he sends his troops to roust you out of house and home. I wonder if my laughter, and that of other women, is a similar whistling in the dark. Are we trying to find this men's movement funny so that we are less frightened by the sight of groups of men together, impassioned and stripping themselves of polite conventions? In another context, they look and sound too much like the gangs of boys that have intimidated and raped us all through recorded time.

One emotion that I have not explored is sadness. And I am sad, a little bit, because it seems that white heterosexual men need a movement; they need groups like the National Organization for Men Against Sexism, the struggling survivor of the antisexist men's movement of the 1970s, home of Stoltenberg and others like him. They *are* destroying themselves and the things that they profess to love through their continued participation in patriarchy. Men need to think together, powerfully and out loud, about how this thing called "masculinity" is highly socially constructed, and therefore can be dethroned at any time in favor of definitions that do not rely upon hierarchies of power and dominance, do not, as Phyllis Chesler pointed out in *About Men*, define war and the destruction of life as the epitome of maleness. For if women are essentially defined as birth-and-life-givers, then men, in Western culture's dichotomous mode, must define themselves as the opposite, as death-dealers. Men need a movement in which they will criticize these tendencies in one another, in which they become the allies of women rather than competing with us over who is more truly the victim of patriarchy.

I'm sad because I doubt that this will happen. The mythopoetic men's movement is likely to go the way of other passions that have swept white middle-class men at times of economic crisis and social and cultural transition; some parts of it will integrate into the general culture, some will disappear, some reemerge in twenty years time as if they were born anew (remember Charles Reich and *The Greening of America?* Same tune, only slightly different words). Some, mostly heterosexual, women will have their hopes for men raised and dashed again. Some women, like myself, will return to our tasks of trying to make the feminist revolution happen one life at a time. A few group leaders and workshop promoters will have made a good living. But saddest of all, this movement will not move us, as a culture. It will leave patriarchy unchallenged and intact. When I come to the end of my analysis, sadness predominates, sadness that all of this energy will go for naught toward genuine change in this wounded world.

LAURA S. BROWN, PH.D. *is a clinical psychologist in the independent practice of feminist therapy and feminist forensic psychology in Seattle, Washington. Her previous writing and lectures have been primarily in the fields of ethics, theory, and practice of feminist therapy, antiracism and multiculturalism in feminist therapy, and psychotherapy with lesbians. She sees her role as one of subverting patriarchy from within while trying to keep it from subverting her.*

A Helping Hand
from the Guys

Vicki Noble

MEN ARE GATHERING in the woods to do ritual, find themselves, bond with each other, and generally re-create themselves after the model set by women over the last two decades. This seems hopeful. I've been aware that men close to feminist women have felt a little lost and left out when we gather together in female-only space. At my speaking engagements, men (or sometimes women) ask me, "What about men? What can we do? How can we be a part of what women are experiencing? Can men be close to the Goddess?" Some men have talked about a "new model of masculinity" that deliberately diverges from the patriarchal, mechanistic one in which they were raised.

But then I started to get worried. What has emerged from the news media and the plethora of recent books written by Robert Bly, Sam Keen, and their younger protégés, is a clearly stated antifeminist backlash. I have hesitated to use a phrase like "men's movement" to describe the track of a few very vocal (and arrogant) men. It's no surprise that the media has so quickly picked up on a "movement" of white men that affirms and reestablishes the traditional male-dominant values of Western patriarchal culture. The women's

101

movement has been active for twenty years, and *Time*, *Newsweek*, and NBC have yet to ask its leading theorists what they actually *think*. Yet the "men's movement" (an infant by comparison) has received full-out coverage from all of these media vehicles, and even alternative ones like *Yoga Journal*. Some of it involves ridicule, of course, but more often, the men are taken quite seriously.

I've been watching the thing grow into a kind of monster, wondering what could possibly be the correct response, since anything critical coming from feminist women is going to add fuel to the fire of the wild men. However, I am now very much reassured about the solution. It is men themselves—bright, clear-thinking, feminist-oriented, and morally outraged men—who are taking it upon themselves to correct the false media impression that there is anything new or (r)evolutionary about the self-aggrandized men's movement. Smart men who have learned that they don't need to separate themselves from the feminine in order to be free have begun to respond to the misogyny in Bly's and Keen's analyses. Men who care about women don't want to be associated with backlash. They've been working too hard in their own lives redressing the "battle of the sexes." Outraged at the infantile remarks of their brothers, they are raising critical voices against their own kind. Peter Murphy, for example, in reviewing Bly's *Iron John* for the popular men's magazine, *Changing Men*, provokes and challenges men by calling Bly's vision "too easy, too mystical, too fundamentally reactionary to bring us anywhere but backwards to an image of masculinity which is not only old, but worn out."[1]

The calm, clear voice of Steve Greaves responding to a *Yoga Journal* feature-spread on the men's movement was also refreshing, and I found myself beginning to relax. Greaves takes responsibility as a man, discussing the use of the phrase "male-bashing" as a "self-justifying, reactive, male sexist term similar to white racists' favorite legalism, 'reverse discrimination.' . . . Rape, pornography, femicide, and other hate crimes against women have been increasing since 1980. Women are more in danger from men they know than our soldiers are from 'enemies' on the battlefield!" Sam Keen (in *Yoga Journal*) had made the ludicrous proposal that women are *equally* responsible with men for the present state of the world, with its wars, crime, and violence. Greaves states the obvious: "Men have ruled all major institutions for millennia, defining masculinity *and* femininity to legitimize men's competitive power-striving, wars of conquest and domination of nature and women."[2]

After my letter appeared suggesting that men might help women in our effort to survive the violence against us,[3] I received a call from a professor working on an article about violence against women to be published in the *Journal of Humanistic Psychology*. Dr. David Elkins wanted to quote from my letter and sent me a draft of his essay. Again I felt very hopeful. Although Elkins is supportive of the men's movement, he challenges men to "confront their own personal shadow in regard to violence," using some of their "newfound 'fierceness' in the service of protecting women from men's violence." Elkins says that men who see the men's movement as an opportunity to oppose women are simply practicing revenge against women based on the false assumption that men and women are equally matched in power.[4]

Similarly, in *Magical Blend*, Will Roscoe, author of *The Zuni Man-Woman*, calls the masculinity that the men's movement is trying to redeem "simply the idealized masculinity of patriarchy," and says, "A lot of the men's movement focuses on the longing for a male authority in our lives to overcome being enveloped and smothered by the mother. That's a paranoid fantasy. Women don't have the power in this culture to do that to men." He suggests that instead of men going out on a hero's journey of some kind, getting away from women, they need instead to "embrace the woman inside of us." Roscoe doesn't think it's the father who can teach that (the men's movement has tended to focus on the "lost father"), but "strong women" who can point the way. He suggests instead that it is not the personal father who influences men today, but the male peer group, the "Old Boy" network a guy hangs out with. "Men need to be weaned from other men, which is why the whole thrust of the Bly-Keen men's movement to go off somewhere with other men to learn how to be men is scary to me."[5]

Steven O'Shea writes: "Some time ago, after reading Robert Bly's best-selling *Iron John: A Book About Men*—or maybe it was Sam Keen's best-selling *Fire in the Belly: On Being a Man*—I realized that I was being cruelly oppressed. Industrial civilization, the rat race, misogyny, racism, cable TV—sure, I created them, but now they're cramping my style." So he goes to France, where he tells us the 1992 Men's Movement Convention will be held, to "penetrate" into the central chamber of a paleolithic cavern there, where there are "paintings of my prey: mammoths, horses, bison, reindeer. *Aaarrghh! Aaarrghhh!* Me want kill! Me want eat! Me want—A guide taps me on the shoulder. 'Have you noticed, m'sieur, that the animals represented are female and most of them are pregnant?'" she asks, and the rest of the tale unfolds from this paradoxical twist.[6]

I am grateful when men step in and do the right thing. I have been putting out this challenge (or plea) to the men I know for sometime now. I first tried it out on my husband, when I was still living with him. He came home one night and found me reading the issue of the new *Ms. Magazine* that focused on violence against women.[7] I was in a state of upset, and I began to pour this out. He reacted immediately, asking me why I was "attacking him," when he had been working hard all day and didn't have anything to do with the rape and murder of women. "Help," I repeated with tears streaming down my face, really getting into the feeling of it. "We need help! Women have been working on this problem for twenty years. We have taken karate classes, started rape crisis centers and domestic shelters for abused women and children; we have worked with the cops, the lawyers, the courts; we have done all kinds of work to empower ourselves and our children. And the only visible response during that time is that the violence against women has increased to proportions that can only be seen as a holocaust!" He stared at me uncertainly and asked what he could possibly do to help. I suggested he talk about it, every day, wherever he was—that he start making people deal with it—and he agreed to do this.

This is what I want from men, and this is exactly what men are beginning to do. I have had a hunch for several years that in the same way that women have awakened to our instinctual birthing and protective abilities in relation to children, that men must also have species instincts toward the protection of women and children as a group. Although some very progressive men's groups have been speaking and acting against rape (most frequently they are gay men), for most men the issue hasn't seemed related to them until now. Now they are responding instinctually, just as I had hoped, but it is coming about as a result of other men embarrassing them by including them in a philosophy they cannot support. They don't want to be associated with antifeminism and a blatant denial of patriarchal reality. These men are—by their actions and their words—creating coalition with women, and with feminist women no less! In our time, with the constant barrage of pressure on men to keep playing they roles that have kept the culture going, this act of alliance takes courage.

So I pretty much ignore the "men's movement," focusing instead on the real work of creating a world that might be fit to live in. Women are working to stop the destruction of the planet, and we're committed for the long haul. I'm interested in brothers who are joined with us in this endeavor, which must necessarily include stopping the war on women and children. This time we're living through is critical. There is reason to hope we will not make ourselves extinct, but it will require that we join together as cells in the one body of our Mother and fight for Her survival. We can't do this when men are in denial about most women's terrifying reality: imprisoned in the cage of the patriarchal family, with rape and murder a constant threat, and no safe place to go to get away.

I remember reading about a survey asking men what they were most afraid of from women, and women what they were most afraid of from men, which revealed a shocking discrepancy between the sexes. Women responded that they feared being raped and murdered, and men responded that they feared being laughed at. How estranged we are from one another, I thought as I read this, as though the sexes lived in two totally different worlds. I wonder how it is that we are able to communicate at all? When men stand up for women against other men more traditional and/or oppressive than themselves, they risk censure and blackball from the Old Boy's Network. But through that action, they break down the barrier that has been erected between the sexes and make union happen. In union there is always healing.

I have a vision of us joining hands together and raising our voices in a great call for justice. I hear us drumming and singing, setting up a sacred rhythm that will heal us and our planet, raising our vibration and making possible a miracle or a healing. As mostly white Westerners, members of the feminist movement and the men's movement have a responsibility to respond to the global situation in an effective way right now, without another wasted moment. I see that our ability to make authentic community together is the key to healing, and that the ego separations between women and men (not to mention gays and straights, Christians and pagans, and all the other schisms between us) must be overcome and abandoned long enough for us to sound a new note, a new intention, on the planet.

I have long maintained that men and patriarchy aren't the same thing, and that real masculinity is an unexplored phenomenon whose time has come. I encourage men to step out from their blanket identification with patriarchy and stand up for what they believe and know themselves to be. When men disassociate themselves from patriarchal roles and expectations and can begin to relate to women authentically, they will have natural impulses to stop the constant rape and murder that our culture simply takes for granted. When men stand up to other men and say, "No more rape!" then the consensus reality in society can change. We can begin to say, collectively, that we do not condone violence against women, and that murder and rape are not okay with us as a culture and as a species.

This is the awakening of sanity and the necessary unification that precedes transformation.

It may be naive, but I can imagine a mass awakening of our consciousness that would make pornography obsolete, because the assumptions behind it no longer exist, having evaporated in the clear light of seeing "the other." I can imagine forgiveness happening on a mass level, opening our hearts and cleansing each of us of the hatred and resentment we feel toward the opposite sex. I can imagine that mass drumming and singing songs of the soul might open our poor mechanized bodies to instinctual, free movement, and our straitjacketed minds to expanded states of awareness that can begin to comprehend the Mystery. I can truly imagine us letting go of the judgments and grievances we have held in relation to one another, and to the belief systems and blind allegiances that have imprisoned us in limited Western cultural ideologies.

Mickey Hart—drummer for the Grateful Dead and author of two new books on world drumming phenomena—in his cross-cultural research into drumming around the world came across the idea that humans have used rhythm in a sacred way for as long as we have existed. But in fact, it may be rhythm itself that differentiated us as human way back at the break between the ape ancestor and who we have become. What a concept! As a healer myself using drumming and chanting to support hands-on healing in a group context with cancer patients, I know the power of the drum-induced rhythm that puts us into trance (an altered state of consciousness) and transports us (as a group, *as one organism*) to a state of ecstasy that heals and transforms—on a *physical* level!

Even cancer, in the process of rapidly taking over the body and killing all the normal cells by its abnormal growth, can suddenly and simply go away. This is called "spontaneous remission," and is not understood by doctors or science. But I've seen it happen as a direct response to a group session of drumming, chanting, and raising heat through hands-on healing. It doesn't always happen, and I don't know how to force it to happen, but the fact that it sometimes happens is enough for me to continue to do the work. And I see that the drumming and healing don't do anything to "kill" the cancer cells, but simply awaken and activate the healthy cells in the body, which then begin to vibrate at a higher frequency and do what they had forgotten how to do. We white Western men and women are like potentially healthy cells who have forgotten how to vibrate. Unlike tribal people all over the world, we don't drum, we don't dance, and we don't touch each other in healing ways, regularly, as a community.

Western women hide our monthly bleeding and have epidemic PMS, and Western men go to war (or to the office) to mechanically prove their potency. Our whole society is sleeping, as if hypnotized by the boring, repetitious litanies of patriarchal culture. The feminist movement has awakened some women to what is natural and should be granted freely, and through our association with the Goddess—an ancient, pervasive image of female sacredness—we have begun to imagine ourselves powerfully enough to risk changing. The men's movement is almost certainly an effort by men to awaken in the same way and toward the same end. I'm glad white men are going to the woods to drum and dance and cry. But I hate it that they blame women for their dilemma, and I wish they would stop making trite analyses that come from their feeling that feminism is going to rob them of their (illegitimate) power and privilege.

There is cancer in this body, and it's raging right now, threatening to annihilate all life on this planet through its blind and very rapid growth. We—all of us—are cells in the larger body of our planet, our Mother Earth. Some are cancer cells, some are healthy cells; it is important to take a stand. Now is the moment of life and death, the perfect opportunity to throw off the cancer, by aligning with the rhythm of the drumbeat, the heartbeat, the planetary immune system. It's time to make coalition, when a body can respond to a survival thrust from within it, the immune system wakes up and throws off the invading illness or virus, and the organism returns to health. I believe there is a strong survival thrust happening in the body of this planet at this time, and that as cells in the larger body, we can respond. One of the worst obstacles to our unification has been the "war between the sexes" that is at the core of patriarchal culture.

The men's movement that interests me is the one that's moving in response to life, knowing that life gestates in and through the Mother, whose very being is organized around sustaining and protecting future generations. I have faith that the growth of the men's movement—because it is generating an instinctual response from healthy cells—will help to turn the tide in this collective fight for time. The destruction of life on the planet has reached the point of no return, like sand running out of the hour glass. Let's leave no one out of our transformation, trusting that anybody can snap at any moment, becoming part of the solution instead of the problem. There is a rhythm, like the beat of a drum, I can hear it and it makes me want to move, with you, with Her, to ecstasy and remembering and renewal.

Notes

1. Peter F. Murphy, "Iron John: A Book About Men," *Changing Men,* Fall/Winter 1991, p. 51.
2. Steven Greaves, "Letters to the Editor," *Yoga Journal,* Sept.–Oct. 1991, p. 16.
3. Vicki Noble, "Letters to the Editor," *Yoga Journal,* Sept.–Oct. 1991, p. 14.
4. David Elkins, "Stopping the Violence Against Women: One Agenda Item for the Men's Movement" (unpublished manuscript).
5. Jerry Snider, "The Zuni Man/Woman: Native America's Third Gender: An Interview with Will Roscoe," *Magical Blend,* January 1992, p. 42.
6. Steven O'Shea, "Insight," *Elle,* November 1991.
7. *Ms.* Magazine, Vol. 1, No. 2, Oct.–Nov. 1990.

VICKI NOBLE *is a feminist shaman healer, cocreator of the* Motherpeace Tarot *and author of* Motherpeace: A Way to the Goddess *(1983). She published two issues of a periodical,* Snakepower: A Journal of Contemporary Female Shamanism, *now becoming an annual book to be published by HarperSanFrancisco, and most recently authored* Shakti Woman: Feeling Our Fire, Healing Our World (The New Female Shamanism) *(1991). She teaches and travels internationally, working with women, healing, and empowerment.*

Men in Feminist Struggle—The Necessary Movement

bell hooks

THOUGH CONTEMPORARY feminist movement continues to serve as a catalyst enabling many women to transform our lives, providing new paradigms for change in how we think about gender and how we act, it is obvious that the vast majority of men remain unmoved by feminist thought or action. Much of the feminist theory addressing men specifically fails to creatively revision and reconceptualize masculinity. There are no books that adequately serve as maps providing males of all ages with a feminist education by explaining what patriarchy is, how it works, and why they should be committed to a feminist movement that opposes sexism and sexist oppression. Male advocates of feminist movement have not made educating masses of men in feminist thought a central political agenda. This is one of the major failings of the contemporary men's movement.

The earliest writings of the men's movement expressed far more concern with dismantling patriarchy and eradicating male domination of women and children than more recent work. There is a sharp contrast between the early collection of essays *For Men Against*

Sexism, edited by Jon Snodgrass in 1977, and the more recent book by John Stoltenberg, *Refusing to Be a Man.* While both men introduce their work by talking about being challenged by individual women to critique male domination, Snodgrass's language is deeply political, while Stoltenberg emphasizes the personal. In the first book, there is always the recognition that men involved with feminist movement must continually critique their motivation, strategies, etc. This emphasis on critical self-interrogation is absent in recent writings from the men's movement. Today's men's movement is much more self-congratulatory.

Without perceiving himself as in any way disloyal to the men's movement, Snodgrass could write: "To understand my own reaction to the women's movement I read feminist literature and searched for materials written by men. . . . I continued my search for a meaningful men's group and helped form the Los Angeles Men's Collective in October 1974. In my practice I heard the men's movement criticized for being 'subjectivists,' 'individualistic,' and 'bourgeois.' I also heard radical males criticized for being 'masculine-identified' and 'dogmatic.' Both criticisms seemed correct to me." These criticisms resonate as I read again the introduction to *Refusing to Be a Man,* wherein Stoltenberg writes: "I count myself part of the struggle for women's equality for reasons that are intensely personal—so personal, sometimes, they can't be glibly declared." Passages like this one are not aimed at educating masses of men about the significance of men's role in feminist struggle. Though Stoltenberg has been for some time a powerful advocate for feminist causes, his writing hints at the kind of estrangement from the political task of feminist education that is potentially the most powerful contribution men can make in feminist movement. And Stoltenberg represents the radical edge of men's movement. The aspect of the men's movement advocated by males like Robert Bly rarely addresses the issue of dismantling patriarchy. Instead, the focus of this branch of the men's movement seems to be more on the production of a kind of masculinity that can be safely expressed within patriarchal boundaries. It emerges more as a critical response to feminism than as a critical commentary on patriarchy.

Ideally, men's movement should merely be a segment under the larger feminist movement. By acting as though such movement exists apart from women's movement, men undermine support for feminist struggle. When feminism is defined as a movement to end sexism and sexist oppression, it is clear that everyone has a role to play. Fundamentally, the struggle is not defined as a conflict between women and men. It is defined by resistance to a politic of patriarchal domination that is perpetuated and maintained by nearly everyone in our culture. Defined in this way, there is no question that men can engage fully in feminist struggle. Unfortunately, as long as individuals both within and outside feminist movement consider it to be a movement for women only or even one that primarily benefits females, men will be allowed to believe that feminist struggle is not for or about them. And it is. It has to be, or patriarchy and male domination will never be eradicated.

The most frightening aspect of contemporary men's movement, particularly as it is expressed in popular culture, is the depoliticization of the struggle to end sexism and sexist oppression, and the replacing of that struggle with a focus on personal self-actualization. Feminist struggle should enhance the male quest for self-actualization. Contemporary men's movement often pits the two against one another, sometimes to such an extent that feminism appears to be seen as the enemy and women the group to be resisted or attacked. The book *King, Warrior, Magician, Lover: Rediscovering the Archetypes of the Mature Masculine* by Robert Moore and Douglas Gillette (who dedicate the work to Robert Bly) is an example of the kind of contemporary focus on masculinity that is utterly depoliticized. In the conclusion to the book, the authors write: "In this book we have been concerned about helping men to take responsibility for immature forms of masculinity. At the same time it is clear that the world is overpopulated with not only immature men but also tyrannical and abusive little girls pretending to be women. It is time for men—particularly the men of Western civilization—to stop accepting the blame for everything that is wrong in the world." Obviously, this statement was not meant to encourage men to assume greater responsibility for their participation in the perpetuation and maintenance of male domination, of sexist thought and action. And indeed there is an implied critique of that aspect of feminist movement that rightly sees men as directly accountable for their continued support of patriarchy.

In the anthology *For Men Against Sexism,* Snodgrass called attention to that aspect of men's movement that grew out of male outrage at women for calling out the evils of patriarchy and naming all men as complicit. Those men who did not see themselves as complicit wanted then, as well as now, to deny male power and male domination or their abusive use of that power. Often they see themselves solely as victims of patriarchy and want to be seen as just as oppressed as any woman. While they positively insist on the need for men to grow emotionally and express feelings, they do not suggest that these actions alone cannot be viewed as meaningful resistance to patriarchy and male domination. Within popular culture in the United States there was and is the stereotypical assumption that men who support feminist movement represent "wimp masculinity." This notion emerged because so many of the males in the men's movement acted as though the most central aspect of the movement for them was the emphasis on opening up, sharing emotions, expressing, crying together. The current use of the term "snag" (sensitive new age guy) to describe these men hints at the narcissism that emerges when males in the men's movement are obsessed primarily with their desire for a safe space for certain forms of personal interaction that are not affirmed in most locations in our society; i.e., a place where men can hug one another, cry, and tell their stories, offering physical and emotional care.

All women active in feminist movement recognize the importance of males learning how to express a wide range of emotions. Yet many of us know from having lived or worked with "snags" that often these men dominate even as they take time to cry, share feelings, and so on. Being a "sensitive new age guy" often serves self-centered male goals. There is little material in the published written work of the contemporary men's movement focusing on ways men can learn to express feelings, emotion, in encounters with women, both private and public, without reinscribing male domination.

Much of the relational focus of contemporary men's movement is aimed at improving homosocial bonding between men. Yet one of the major dilemmas created by sexism and sexist oppression is the inability of men to bond with women in all aspects of social life. Until the men's movement focuses more on unlearning sexism and sexist practices as they are acted out in everyday life, it will not have the full support of feminist women, or actively challenge the status quo.

My most immediate experience of the "men's movement" occurred when I attended one of the major conferences focusing on men who are concerned with confronting sexism and challenging patriarchy and heterosexism. I must confess with all honesty that I did not feel "safe" at this conference. Many males articulated their desire that women not be present and some that even those of us who were invited speakers not be allowed to speak. Some men explained their resentment of female presence by saying that this was their "special" time away from women. I kept thinking if this celebration of homosocial male bonding could only take place as a re-action against the female and if the men present were supposedly more conscious than most men of sexism in our society, then there was not a lot of hope that men would ever participate fully in feminist movement. Many of the men present seemed not to understand that the contempt and disdain that they were expressing for female presence was akin to that expressed by misogynist and/or sexist men, and their denial of the link between the two seemed dangerous. In some ways this conference mirrored early radical feminist meetings where male presence was not tolerated or desired but with one difference. Homosocial bonding (men strengthening their bonds with one another), albeit on different terms, is promoted and affirmed constantly in this society. Should a men's movement exist that is primarily concerned with intensifying male interest and pleasure in homosocial bonding?

I came to the conference with a black male who has been and is a supportive colleague though we teach at different places. A gay black man with a white lover, he had not attended such an event before and felt after attending that all he could say was "never again." We were both disturbed by the complete lack of any emphasis on race. We were disturbed by the discussions of masculine identity that were based on the assumption that all men share equally the rewards of patriarchal privilege in this society. Privileged white male thought, experience, and culture was often presented as a norm standpoint. There were few black men present. And there was no real emphasis on outreach. It was definitely (as some all female feminist gatherings and conferences have been) an exclusive meeting for the "in" crowd. There was no indication of the way in which progressive ideas about gender, about masculinity, even would be shared with an audience beyond those able to attend the conference. While I met individual men at the conference who were deeply committed to the struggle to end sexism, in general the issues of patriarchy and abusive male domination of women and children were not the central agenda. Indeed, it appeared as though feminist movement had somehow been appropriated and made to serve the interest of creating an alternative space for men to gather without any apparent sustained commitment to feminist movement. Where is the work within contemporary men's movement that affirms the struggle to end sexism and sexist oppression? To what extent has the focus on male woundedness (healing the child within), which is an important process of self-actualization, obscured the need for organized collective resistance?

In all my feminist writing, I have labored to articulate the deeply felt conviction that men must play an active role in feminist struggle. While I am critical of those aspects of the men's movement that render it less than radical, not a political space for men to educate for feminist critical consciousness and work at transforming society, there is no doubt in my mind that there must be such a movement. In its present form much of the men's movement is presented to the public as being a response to the demasculinization of men. And feminism is often seen as one of the "weapons" women have used to belittle men. As long as sexist and/or misogynist sentiments inform the core belief system within men's movement, feminist struggle is undermined. I know of no instance where men have come to women within feminist movement to request critical feedback about the direction of the men's movement. This is unfortunate. For in many ways the same forces that have undermined women-centered feminist movement are undermining the men's movement. Let me reiterate that we need a men's movement that is part of revolutionary feminist movement. If the masses of men in our society have not unlearned their sexism, have not abdicated male privilege, then it should be obvious that a men's movement led only by men with only males participating runs the risk of mirroring in a different form much that is already oppressive in patriarchal culture. Much of what Bly and his followers offer as an affirmation of a different masculinity is only a nineteenth-century notion of the benevolent patriarch. Currently contemporary men's movement does not address in a serious political manner feminist transformation of society. Until the men's movement renews its connection with revolutionary feminist struggle in such a manner that efforts to end sexism and sexist oppression remain central agendas, it will lend itself to cooptation by the status quo. Men active in feminist struggle, in the men's movement, need at this historical juncture to pause and reevaluate the direction of their work, asking themselves whose interests are served in the men's movement? How and in what concrete ways does the men's movement advance feminist struggle? These questions need to be answered if we are to build the kind of political solidarity between women and men that shows by example that feminist thought and practice liberates us all.

---

bell hooks is *Associate Professor of English and Women's Studies at Oberlin College. A feminist theorist, cultural critic, and creative writer, she is the author of* Ain't I a Woman, Feminist Theory: From Margin to Center, Talking Back, Yearning: Race, Gender, and Cultural Politics. *Her most recent book, written in collaboration with Cornel West, is* Breaking Bread: Insurgent Black Intellectual Life, *all published by South End Press.*

The Men's Movement of Choice

Kathleen Carlin

I WORK IN AN organization created to stop men from battering women. While it is a place where men work together in groups to stop their own and others' battering, the organization's primary mission is to end male violence against women. This mission, simple as it sounds, was the object of some debate during the early years of our organization. Why should the goal be to eliminate violence against women rather than to help the batterers, since that is the actual work that we do? After all, the argument went, if you help men stop battering, you're helping the victims.

I'm not sure why I was surprised at the intense resistance to putting victims' safety first. I know that to put women's interests ahead of men's so fundamentally violates the status quo that we all react with terror and confusion at the thought. Women know that to put women's interests ahead of men's makes women a more prominent target for men's rage. We, as women, feel safer with what Martin Dufresne calls the "trickle down" model for ending violence: We would prefer to treat the symptoms of that violence and hope for the best than to call attention to the deeply embedded ideology of male supremacy that sanctions it.

But just as trickle down economics is a strategy designed ultimately to keep money and control of it just where it is, so the strategies we use to challenge male violence against women, which enforces and maintains male supremacy, won't be effective without dismantling male supremacy and the oppression of women. And as long as men's relationships with others are held in place by the abuse of power and control, masculinity itself will of necessity be a hollow identity—a demon haunting men rather than the fulfillment of humanness.

The mythopoetic men's movement, if it has done nothing else, has thrown into public discourse a picture of the dis-ease among men with "masculinity"—at least among those men who have the privilege to be self-aware and to talk about it, and bring it into the mass culture. The spokesmen for this movement have captured the sense of this dis-ease, they have given it voice and a prescription for a catharsis of sensory relief, but they make no demands for change in the underlying structures causing their malaise. As a member of the class of people designated to be subordinate in a male supremacist society, I watch with curiosity and apprehension as these men approach the search for the "true masculine" as something denied them. I would like to say something about how that makes me nervous.

When speaking about male dominance and the oppression of women, it is not only tempting, it's easy, to see men as victims, too. In patriarchy, men have had to live as members of a group engaged in upholding a structure of dominance, whether any individual chose that or not. The same social order that organized itself around men owning women and children had to order men into hierarchies as well. These dominant-subordinate relationships among men have been based on class, race, religion, sexual orientation, or other factors. Therefore, most men have lived in positions of subordination to other men, often enforced by violence. And so, one can say, some men are victimized, not by women, as the right-wing men's movement says, but by other men. One can use this logic to justify focusing on defining and reworking those dominant-subordinate relationships between men, such as the mythopoetics' focus on father-son relations and male bonding.

A basic problem with this approach, and with the mythopoetic men's movement as a whole, is that it moves within the aura of that guiding principle of patriarchy: that male nature characterizes full humanity, that men are central, the core around which all others revolve. Therefore, men getting together with men to struggle with feelings, identity, and relationship seems substantial, paramount, imminently worthwhile. Within this worldview, the problems and pain of women are infinitely less interesting, less compelling, less urgent, than those of men.

In patriarchy, men are located in such a way as to have virtually total and exclusive access to the entire range of resources available within society, resulting in what is operationally a male homosocial world—where men are attracted to, stimulated by, and interested in other men, even though that attraction may be characterized by fear and competition. In such a world, itself characterized by territoriality, dominance, resource acquisition, and loyalty, men can satisfy their needs from other men. In this world, women become resources that men can use to further their own eminence. Women are excluded, not because they are competitors, but because they are deemed irrelevant.

An earlier focus of this men's movement encouraged men to develop their "feminine" side by cultivating such qualities as emotionality, gentleness, and nurturing. Yet the attribution of these basic human characteristics as "female" was an arbitrary nineteenth-century construction designed to emphasize women's difference from and inferiority to men. When a man espouses this view, I hear this: I think I can actually override my devaluing of women sufficiently to appropriate those "feminine" qualities that will make me a more complete person. I hear this as an attempt to appropriate some exotic artifact that will enhance, enlarge upon his image of himself—and, as a woman, I begin to feel like the witch doctor's mask hanging on his wall.

Surely one reason for the enthusiasm welcoming the current men's movement must be that its ideology not only gives men permission to abandon the attempts to develop their feminine sides, but more than that offers an ideology actually incorporating the irrelevancy of women. What a relief it must be to be able to think about, play with, and abound in "masculinity" without ever having to bother with the fact that its very existence relies solely on the construction of that to which it is opposed: the other, the shadow, the inferior, to be warded off, to be better than, and superior to. This is only a recycled version of imperialism: man, standing above and apart from nature, who in solitude controls and dominates it while pursuing some ancient impulse to be rejoined with it. Women exist only to mirror back the centrality of men.

The solution is neither for men to develop their "feminine" sides, nor to fetishize the "masculine" with the calling forth of the inner "wild man." The solution is to deconstruct a masculinity that is founded on not-being-a-woman, on woman-hating. (By "woman-hating, I do not mean the *Hustler* magazine kind. I mean simply the attitude that male nature is held to be expressive of full humanity. And when men say to me, "That's not woman-hating," I say, "I rest my case.")

This solution means to give up, really give up, male dominance—there's no having it both ways. It means departing from that androcentric, homosocial world where men talk to men about men and come up with some variation of the old solutions that maintain male centrality and dominance. Instead, it will mean not only to engage in activities that cultivate growth and enhancement in others along with oneself, it will mean relating to women as peers whose basic worth and way of being in the world are recognized as fully as men's. It means that women enter the process of history making as themselves, as subjects, determining and directing an equal share of the human discourse.

How to do such a thing? How does one start? How do we step outside a history, a language, and a social order that inform our every decision? One place to begin is to listen to those who have been marginalized, who have been placed outside the center of history. Women's stories, told from our own subjective reality, reveal a context in which men might start to address the real source of their dis-ease with the experience of masculinity. But this process is easier said than done, for in telling our own stories, women stop functioning as mirrors of men's centrality. Men experience this act as life-threatening; they are driven back upon themselves. The ground on which they stand and have their being is shaken. They experience an existential not-knowing. It's no surprise that they react strongly, even violently. And in that moment, they have a choice.

To the men in our batterers' groups, it is then that someone says to him that he has a choice. He can either do more of what he's done—more threats, more pressure, more intimidation to put her "in her place," or he can risk hearing her and sitting with it until he begins to understand what a new response would be. To sit in the midst of that not-knowing bespeaks fundamental uncertainty, an untenable position for men for whom a sense of control is essential. But the batterer who can transverse that time of not-knowing begins the journey toward a new life. His own personal house of cards has fallen, but he now has access to the tools to build a new house, one founded on love instead of power, freedom instead of control, liberation instead of oppression.

For the men's movement, searching for a healthy experience of maleness, this moment of choice is no less dramatic or unsettling. The decision to give up male centrality, to listen to those who have been marginalized, to be willing to perceive a broader, richer reality than male supremacy offers, means giving up all forms of controlling and abusive behaviors and learning new skills with which to negotiate the intricate, demanding transition that lies ahead.

To imagine what is possible, I would like to call forth the famous Gestalt illustration of what is obviously a white vase on a black background. If we study it long enough, a shift in perception occurs and we find ourselves seeing, instead, two faces in profile facing each other. Suddenly the vase, so prominent in our first look, has become background for the faces. We find we can now see two pictures: the white vase, for which the black is ground, or two faces in profile, for which the white is ground. Each is figure, each is ground, but never at the same time. But now that we have recognized and given value to both images, we are able to move back and forth between them at will. In the same way, when men recognize and give value to women's experience, they gain the skill of seeing broader possibilities for human existence. They create the opportunity to make a choice.

Using the genre of fairy tales so important to the mythopoetic movement, this is a story where an evil monster casts a spell over the people, keeping everyone suspended until finally the hero dares to confront the monster and break the spell. We are all kept spellbound by the ideology of male supremacy as the natural order, ordained in creation. Exposing the monster's false power, thus breaking the spell, happens when a man dares to enter the realm of women's reality. A man breaks rank with other men when they make women's reality their referrant. All the power of the social order gathers itself to prevent his going there.

A man who dares this act defects from the homeland of patriarchy. The defector knows he can no longer live in this home, so he gives up position, status, and possessions, slipping off under cover of night for an unfamiliar destination. He betrays those who have trusted him to remain true to an idea, a place, a collective identification. Where he is going, he risks being regarded with suspicion, of not being readily accepted, because of what he has left. He makes his choice from the private knowledge that patriarchy is killing him, too, as it is killing others. He understands that to save himself means not grasping the patriarchy closer, but letting it die—even the part of it that resides within himself.

KATHLEEN CARLIN *grew up in Nebraska. An activist in the battered women's movement, she directed a shelter for battered women for six years, and speaks and writes on issues of violence toward women, men who batter, and feminism. She is a founding board member and former chair of the National Woman Abuse Prevention Center. Since 1985 she has been executive director of Men Stopping Violence. This essay is adapted from a talk presented at the Men and Masculinity Conference in 1990. Soon after that she joined a women's trek that climbed Mt. Kenya. She lives in Atlanta with Jack. Together they are the parents of two wonderful, competent, self-possessed young women, Suzanne and Elizabeth.*

"Father Hunger":
Why "Soup Kitchen"
Fathers Are Not
Good Enough

Myriam Miedzian

"NOT SEEING YOUR father when you are small, never being with him, having a remote father, an absent father, a workaholic father, is an injury," Robert Bly writes in *Iron John* (p. 38). It is a very serious and common injury: Bly tells us that since the early 1980s, at endless men's gatherings, he has heard men state over and over, "in a hundred different ways" that "there is not enough father" (p. 92). He warns that boys who have not had enough fathering will suffer from "father hunger" for the rest of their lives. Searching for the emotional connectedness and sense of masculine identity they never got from their father, "such hungry sons hang around older men like the homeless do around a soup kitchen" (p. 94).

One might expect that Bly's deep awareness of this father hunger, and the pain it causes so many men (including him), would lead him to work on improving the situation. He could do much to help men who look to him for guidance, and are themselves fathers, to become better fathers. He could focus attention on what can be done to change the socialization of today's young boys so that when they grow up those who become fathers will be involved, caring, responsible. At least future generations of men would be spared the suffering.

People who have suffered from a particular problem, or have lost a family member or close friend to drugs, or violent death, or a drunken driver, often find solace and emotional renewal in working toward changes that will prevent the same suffering in others. It seems puzzling then that Bly and other members of the mythopoetic wing of the men's movement have not made this a major focus of their attention. In fact, Bly concludes his discussion of fathering by simply stating that the situation of "too little father . . . is probably not going to get better" (p. 122).

The best Bly seems to offer men now and in the future is second best—the "soup kitchen" of hanging around older men—instead of the real thing, a caring, involved father. He focuses almost exclusively on male initiation rites as the healing path that will restore to fatherless men a sense of connection with men and a sense of their own masculinity. In support of this emphasis, he tells us that in most traditional cultures "old men simply go into the women's compounds with spears one day when the boys are between eight and twelve and take the boys away. Up to that point, the boys have lived exclusively with the women" (p. 86). He gives the example of New Guinea, where the initiated men live together in separate houses and come unannounced to lead the screaming, terrified boys away from their mothers. But Bly ignores anthropological research indicating that it is precisely those societies where little boys are deprived of fathering that have elaborate, often excruciatingly painful, male initiation rites. Anthropologists tell us that when the little boy has only his mother to identify with, then "the initiation rites serve psychologically to brainwash the primary feminine identity and to establish firmly the secondary male identity" (Burton and Whiting, p. 90). In brief, the crisis in male identity is only a problem when the father is not involved in early child rearing, thus depriving his son of a male role model and emotional bond. The research points to another connected problem. While many single mothers succeed in raising fine sons, the fact remains that fatherless boys are at higher risk for antisocial, violent behavior. They often grow up insecure with respect for masculine identity, which can lead to an exaggerated concern with rejecting everything "feminine" and a need to prove masculinity by acting extremely tough, callous, eager to fight. Anthropologists refer to this as "protest masculinity" and sociologists as "hypermasculinity." Bly recognizes this problem. He quotes approvingly a Detroit police chief who points out that "the young men he arrests not only don't have any responsible older man in the house, they have never met one" (p. 32). Since it is clear to Bly and his colleagues that the real problem, on so many levels, is the absence of an involved, nurturant father, why are they so unconcerned with encouraging men to become such fathers?

The likely answer to this question became clear to me when I recently attended a symposium on fatherhood and found that many of the men there were uncomfortable even talking about "nurturant" fathering because this suggests to them that fathers are interchangeable with mothers. One of their major concerns was to differentiate the role of the father from that of the mother, lest fathers lose their "masculinity" and become "effeminate." Since mothers have traditionally been the nurturers and daily caretakers, the father's role must be more distant and more detached, they seemed to be saying. But there was considerable confusion among these men. For while they expressed such views, they also bemoaned the traditional detached father and those who had young children exhibited deep emotional and "nurturant" ties to them. The essence of their conflicted feelings was captured in an anecdote told by one of the men. He described, approvingly, a truck driver he had met who fully shared child care with his wife. Because the truck driver did not define nurturant child care as a primary activity—because he identified himself as a truck driver, not as a nurturant father—his fathering role did not interfere with his masculinity. It seems that many men fear that if they allow themselves to develop traits of nurturance, empathy, and caring, they will lose their male identity. (This reminds one of nineteenth century fears that if women were allowed to go to universities, to think, to work outside the home, they would lose their feminine identity.)

Could it be, then, that Bly and his colleagues are more concerned with proving their "fierceness," which, as they see it, differentiates them as "real men," than they are with encouraging good fathering, which they fear would render them "effeminate"? If so, they are assuming, mistakenly, that a man cannot both be deeply involved in the care of his children and exhibit some of the traits traditionally connected with masculinity. In fact, in a study, when a group of fathers who were primary caregivers were given the BEM Sex Role Inventory, no significant difference emerged between them and the husbands of primary caregiving wives. The BEM test is intended to determine how "masculine," "feminine," or "androgynous" a subject is in very traditional terms. This is not to say that nurturant fathering would leave men unchanged. Nurturing fathers become "more patient, more tuned in, more sensitive to other people's needs," comments a researcher in the field (Ehrensaft, p. 164).

We live at a time when 24 percent of children are growing up without any father in the home, when close to half of divorced fathers never see their children. Rates of violent crime committed by men have soared (over 350,000 Americans have been murdered in the last sixteen years), with many perpetrators coming from fatherless homes. When given the opportunity to get in touch with their feelings, many men spend much of their time bemoaning the lack of fathering they got.

It is disappointing that at a time of such intense crisis, men like Bly are doing so little to remedy the situation.

My own research has led me to conclude that much can be done. Introducing child-rearing classes in all our elementary schools would be a big step in the right direction. When I visited such classes at inner city elementary and upper-class private schools I was amazed at the level of enthusiasm that the young boys exhibited for learning about young children and interacting with them, when given permission to do so. (It is tragic that by the age of about six most boys have learned that anything having to do with babies and child care is "girls' stuff.") These classes sensitize boys and girls to the needs of young children, deter them from child battering, *and encourage young boys to view themselves as future involved, caring, responsible fathers.* They also serve as teenage pregnancy deterrents. Once children learn how demanding and important it is to be a good parent, they become far more inclined to put it off until they are psychologically and financially ready. If we introduced such classes in all our schools by fifth grade at the latest (some girls are getting pregnant by the time they are twelve), and repeated them at a more sophisticated level in high school, we would have far fewer fatherless boys and far more nonviolent, responsible, involved fathers.

While early education is ideal, there are some excellent programs that encourage unwed teenage fathers to get involved emotionally with their children and support them financially. There are programs that help wife and child batterers understand and control their behavior. Legislation such as the Family Leave Bill would enable fathers to spend more time with their young children. It needs strong and broad support.

Surely, the time has come for the mythopoetic wing of the men's movement to take the next step, to move beyond soul searching and the focus on ancient rituals themselves based on the absence of involved fathers and to lend active support to workable, concrete, solutions to the crisis in fathering.

References

Bly, Robert. *Iron John.* Reading, MA: Addison-Wesley, 1991.

Burton, Roger V., and Whiting, John W. M. "The Absent Father and Cross-Sex Identity," *Merrill-Palmer Quarterly* 7 (1961).

Ehrensaft, Diane. *Parenting Together: Men and Women Sharing the Care of Their Children.* New York: The Free Press, 1987.

Professor of Philosophy and journalist MYRIAM MIEDZIAN *holds a Ph.D. in Philosophy from Columbia University. She has also received a Masters in Clinical Social Work from Hunter College,*

the City University of New York. *She is the author of* Boys Will
Be Boys: Breaking the Link Between Masculinity and
Violence. *Her writings on male socialization, the psychology of
criminal behavior, the breakdown of ethical values in contemporary American society, and on a variety of women's issues have
appeared in many publications. Dr. Miedzian has served on the
faculty of Rutgers University and the City University of New
York, and has also taught at Barnard College and the University
of California, San Diego.*

The Men's Auxiliary: Protecting the Rule of the Fathers

Phyllis Chesler

THE MALE LEGAL ownership of children is essential to patriarchy. Women are supposed to breed, bear, and/or socialize father-owned "legitimate" children within a father-absent and mother-blaming family. The fact that fathers are often absent or abusive when present (incestuous, infanticidal, infantile), doesn't change what patriarchy is about—literally, "the rule of the fathers."

I have explored this paradox in each of my books: in *Women and Madness* in 1972 and in *Women, Money and Power* in 1976. In 1978, I did so more mythopoetically in *About Men*. Long before Robert Bly, I saw men as father-wounded sons who therefore grow up to scapegoat women for their fathers' many failings. In *About Men* I said:

> How sad that men would base an entire civilization on the principle of paternity, upon male legal ownership of and presumed responsibility for children, and then never really get to know their sons or their daughters very well; never really participate, for whatever reason, in parenting, in daily, intimate fathering.
>
> True rebellion against a father frightens sons terribly. Sons have just barely begun to overthrow their original parents, their mothers. So I am concerned with displacements of male-male

133

rage and grief onto safe targets, onto weaker men, onto children, onto women.

I viewed male uterus envy as probably the major psychological force behind the patriarchal creation myths (God as a father-creator of humanity) and behind the consequent secular myths that held man as medical expert to be superior to woman as mother. (My Rx for men was not male separatist drum-beating sessions but feminist consciousness and activism.)

So I was not surprised when I first encountered fathers' rights activists in the late 1970s, claiming male maternal superiority and blaming women for fathers' failures. Eventually, I wrote about them in *Mothers on Trial: The Battle for Children and Custody*, in 1986. The collective message presented by "fathers' rights" groups is a chilling one: that children belong to men (sperm donors, surrogate contract fathers, live-in boyfriends, legal husbands) when men want them, but not when men don't. Exactly who and what is the organized men's rights/father's rights movement?

It is patriarchy itself: the church, the state, and private enterprise, as it herds women into sex-typed, lesser lives; it is our own families, sacrificing its female members and defending its male members, even when they're known to have seriously wronged women and children. It is the profound and unending hostility women encounter—on street corners, on dates, at work; it is my own twenty-two-year battle to gain full professorship at my university. The fathers' rights movement is the men's auxiliary to this larger men's movement.

The fathers' rights movement in America grew out of the male feminist movement and the antifeminist new right. What the men's rights movement has done during the past twenty years is to repackage long-standing ideas about father-rights, sometimes in a progressive voice, other times in a reactionary one.

"Left-wing" (or feminist) fathers' rights activists claim that fathers have an equal right to children because men can mother also.

They say that: "Mother is a verb, not a noun," and "A man can be a better mother than a woman can."

"Right-wing" (or patriarchal) fathers' rights activists claim that children need a father-dominated family. They also claim that God is the "father" of all children and that He appointed earthly fathers as "His" children's custodians.

Both kinds of fathers' rights activists share certain perspectives and strategies. They claim that as men they are savagely "discriminated" against by lawyers, judges, and ex-wives in custody matters; that as men they are economically enslaved and controlled by greedy and parasitic ex-wives who prevent them from seeing their children. And they argue that men's parenting—whether on a "mothering" or a patriarchal fathering model—is sufficient and often superior to women's parenting.

There is no comparable movement for mothers' rights—that is, for custody, child support, alimony, marital property, increased levels of welfare, "free" legal counsel upon divorce, and so forth. But there should be because, despite men's movement cries of "unfair," it is in fact mothers' and children's interests that are routinely sacrificed on men's behalf.

In reality, the fathers' rights movement

1. campaigns against abortion rights, and sometimes against female birth control;

2. counsels men to kidnap children, either legally or illegally, and to default on alimony, health, and child-support payments;

3. lobbies against state-initiated actions against "deadbeat dads" and for programs that replace women's rights to a lawyer and a court hearing with mandatory mediation favoring joint legal custody;

4. lobbies the media and state legislatures to dismiss allegations that fathers commit incest (as lies fabricated by vindictive

wives and manipulated children), manipulates anecdotes and social science data (e.g., about "battered husbands"), and demands—and commands—"equal time" in public and media discussions;

5. fails to lobby for health, education, and welfare—a family allowance appropriate to human needs and dignity.

As I began to work actively on behalf of women who were targets of this growing movement, I was surprised when a good number of feminists seemed to support fathers' rights—in the mistaken hope that if we allowed men even more rights than they already had they'd become more responsible and nurturant, at least to their own children; or if we counseled women to give up custody of children that they (and other women) would choose to devote themselves to feminist pursuits instead. In 1979, in *With Child: A Diary of Motherhood*, I wrote about motherhood as a feminist and spiritual pursuit; however, many feminists were not yet interested in motherhood as a *feminist* pursuit.

Feminists have no difficulty uniting around the issue of women's reproductive rights and health. We all understand that the opposition to women's right to control our own bodies is about maintaining men's power. But the issue of "fatherhood" and male parenting has proved to be far more complex and divisive. I have found that my pro-woman position embarrasses and threatens the kind of perfectly good liberal feminist who is not as concerned with a woman's right to choose motherhood when our right to abortion is in such jeopardy; who ardently believes in the *ideal* of male (heterosexual) parenting and joint custody and in the reality of lesbian adoption, and the rights of the lesbian co-mother and adoptive couple over and against the rights of the lesbian biological mother or the nonlesbian, Third World impoverished birth mother; the kind of feminist who views the right to have an abortion or to "choose" noncustodial motherhood as somehow morally and politically superior choices than the right to *retain* custody of the child you chose to have.

I grant that the issue is exceedingly complex and does not lend itself to simplistic solutions. Yet, as I see it, once feminists began fighting for equal pay and for the right to abortion, the backlash was on. If women wanted the right to leave men or take men's jobs away from them, then men, and the women who support them, would simply repossess women's children as well as women's bodies. While feminists, to our credit, may want to be "fair" to men, patriarchs are anything *but* "fair" to women.

Since I examined this new auxiliary backlash in *Mothers on Trial*, first published in 1986, more than five thousand mothers have called or written. "I'm in your book," they say. "It's as if you knew my story personally." Fathers' rights activists, both men and women, do not call or write. Instead, they picket my lectures and threaten lawsuits. In media debates, they literally shout at me, trying to drown out what I have to say. "Why don't you admit it?" they demand. "Ex-wives destroy men economically. They deprive fathers of visitation and brainwash the children against them. Fathers should have rights to alimony and child support. Joint custody should be mandatory. Why do you refuse to see it our way? We've already convinced legislators and lawyers, judges and social workers, psychiatrists and journalists—and many feminists—that what we're saying is true."

Indeed they have. I know about their convictions from firsthand experience. I've been denied employment and threatened with firing, I've been sued by fathers' rights activists, threatened with imprisonment, and received my feminist share of obscene phone calls and death threats. After one particularly harrowing encounter with these activists at a public gathering, I found a dead animal at my door. Early in 1986, for the first time in U.S. history, the FBI convened a grand jury on an ostensibly domestic matter: to question me about the whereabouts of a runaway mother and her two "allegedly" sexually abused children. They had reason to believe I'd helped her. Friends: 1986 was not my favorite year. But in part because of the intense reaction to my work, I've come to think of myself as a freedom fighter or abolitionist opposed to female slavery. I've learned to take myself seriously—not only because others support my views, but also because they oppose them.

What is different about this backlash is that some feminists support it. They argue that the best way to achieve women's liberation is through a "gender neutral" approach—by treating women and men, mothers and fathers, as if they were the same; i.e., all white men and as such, deserving of equality. But men and women, and mothers and fathers, are not equal under patriarchy. The equal treatment of unequals is unjust. And the "gender-neutral" approach often backfires.

In *Mothers on Trial,* I challenge the myth that fit mothers always win custody—indeed, I found that when fathers fight they win custody 70 percent of the time, even when they have been absentee or violent fathers. Since then, other studies have demonstrated that when men fight they win custody anywhere from 50 to 80 percent of the time—whether or not they have been involved in child care or the economic support of the family.

Although 80 to 85 percent of custodial parents are mothers, fathers who fight win custody not because mothers are unfit or because fathers have performed any housework or child care, but because mothers are held to a much higher standard of parenting.

In custody battles, mothers are routinely punished for having a career or job (she's a "selfish absentee mother") *or* for staying home on welfare (she's a "lazy parasite"); for committing heterosexual adultery or for living with a man out of wedlock (she's "setting an immoral example") *or* for remarrying (she's trying to "erase the real dad") *or* for failing to provide a male role model (she's a "bitter, man-hating lesbian").

Divorcing fathers increasingly use the threat of a custody battle as an economic bargaining chip. And it works. He gets the house, the car, and the boat; she gets the kids, and, if she's lucky, minimal child support. When fathers persist, a high percentage win custody because judges tend to view the higher male income and the father-dominated family as in the "best interest of the child." Many judges also assume that the father who fights for custody is rare and should therefore be rewarded for loving his children, or that something is wrong with the mother.

What may be "wrong" with the mother is that she and her children are being systematically impoverished, psychologically and legally harassed, and physically battered by the very father who is fighting for custody. However, mothers are often custodially punished for leaving a violent husband (she's "economically depriving her kids and violating her marriage vows") *or* for staying (she "married him so I hold her responsible for what he did"). Some people, including psychiatrists, lawyers, and judges, deal with male domestic violence by concluding that women have either provoked or exaggerated it.

Coparenting or "male mothering" is an ideal of some feminist theorists, who therefore support joint custody of children as the preferred arrangement after divorce. However, this is liberal theoretics, not scientific fact—and leaders of the joint custody movement such as Dr. Judith Wallerstein are now saying just this. Inviting men to have more involvement in child care, through a joint custody arrangement, will not necessarily produce more "mothering," but perhaps more patriarchal "fathering." The "disconnected" men who have been socialized to reproduce sexism are the very men whom feminists have been calling upon to participate "equally" in child care. Dr. Miriam Johnson, in *Strong Mothers, Weak Wives,* concludes that fathers—not mothers—control and dominate gender stereotyping. She asks: Would not such men "carry their dominating tendencies" into the nursery? Do we really want such men involved in mothering?

I am absolutely in favor of getting men off the battlefields and into the kitchen; and absolutely in favor of male tenderness, intimacy, accountability. However, I am arguing that the call for "gender neutrality" in custodial determination is a mistake. A deeper and closer look at the way "gender neutrality" works in actual custody cases shows that, rather than achieving equality, it may enhance male, patriarchal power, and the primacy of sperm.

The patriarchal ideal of fatherhood is sacred. As such, it usually protects each father from the consequences of his actions. The ideal of motherhood is sacred, too, but no human mother can live up to it, so it serves to expose all mothers as imperfect. Therefore, *all* mothers are custodially vulnerable because they are women; *all* fathers, including incestuous, violent, absent, passive, or "helper" fathers, can win custody, not because mothers are "unfit" or because fathers are truly equal partners, but because fathers are men.

The equal treatment of "unequals" is unjust. In real patriarchy, the paternal demand for "equal" custodial rights, and the law that values legal paternity or male economic superiority over biological motherhood and/or over women's primary care of children, degrades and violates both mothers and children.

(The author would like to acknowledge Ara Wilson's assistance.)

PHYLLIS CHESLER *is a psychologist and the author of six books:* Women and Madness, Women, Money and Power, About Men, With Child: A Diary of Motherhood, Mothers on Trial: The Battle for Children and Custody, *and* Sacred Bond: The Legacy of Baby M. *She is a Professor of Psychology at the College of Staten Island, City University of New York, and the editor-at-large for the feminist magazine* On the Issues. *She is one of the founders of the Association for Women in Psychology, The National Women's Health Network, and an APA Custody Training Institute. She is writing a book on women and self-defense that focuses on the case of the nation's so-called first female serial killer.*

"And So She Walked Over and Kissed Him . . ." Robert Bly's Men's Movement

Margaret Randall

I WILL STATE my position. Although I am not a separatist, I am a lesbian feminist. As the socialist experiments splinter about me, I refuse to relinquish my belief in a society that works for everyone, satisfying our needs and nurturing our creativity regardless of class origin, gender, color, culture, sexual preference, age, abilities. No, not *regardless* of these aspects of our identities, but building upon them, enabling us to contribute to the whole *out of and because of who we are,* with a healthy respect for difference. I am an artist: a writer, photographer, teacher, political activist, mother, grandmother, lover. And I am aware that I live in a time when women's power, reclaimed at enormous personal risk, feels threatening to most men.

The last quarter of the twentieth century has seen a great contemporary rising of the women: once again we have risked what for most was the only life we knew—because we could no longer endure the silence, the beatings, the frozen dreams. This time around, we understand that the practice of re-memory is necessary. And that certain tools are important. One such tool is feminist theory, which helps us to center ourselves in history. Another is feminist therapy, enabling us to reintegrate our feelings at the center of our lives.

Our twentieth century has also seen unloosed the pent-up rage and frustration placed upon women by centuries of gender oppression. Carolyn Heilbrun has written that "to allow oneself . . . the expression of one's feminism is an experience for which there is no male counterpart, at least for white men in the western world."[1] Every time we do, men become threatened, crazed. With the power they have usurped, they punish us; depending upon the time and place they may burn us at the stake, bury us alive with our deceased husbands, or further restrict what control over our lives we may have struggled for and won.

Most men, conditioned to seek their identities in women's eyes, become terrified of all those dark mirrors throwing them back upon their own damaged resources. Some have been able to take leadership from women's wisdom, to look to their own history, to examine feelings. In the last decade, a men's movement has emerged—not, as in the case of the women's movement, in response to societal exploitation and oppression, but rather provoked by the disturbing loss of confidence many men experience when faced with women's gain in strength.

As is true of the women's movement, the men's movement has many faces. Insofar as it encourages men to take a real look at their history, exploitative practices, and resultant personal damage, all to the good. But if it is a movement that serves only to weld shut those cracks that feminism has made in patriarchy, then it is neither good nor particularly new. At least one face of the men's movement, espoused by the poet Robert Bly, seems to embody that which is most brutal and at the same time pathetic about the male ego. In our commodity-based society, a society of the quick fix, I suppose Bly and his fans are unsurprising products of our times.

Bly's appearance on national television[2] as well as his sell-out retreats and best-selling *Iron John: A Book About Men*,[3] have catapulted him to heady fame. To feminists and others who have given serious thought to the way our society divides along gender lines, the Bly phenomenon is simple. A rather blustery old man, an arrogant showman, he has decided he's not taking any more of this *feminist stuff*. That, by golly, he's going to do something about it, maybe even make a living off the project.

So far, so ordinary. We find less-public versions of Bly's Iron John in boardrooms, classrooms, military command posts, and bedrooms around the world. Most women are sincerely concerned that the men in their lives—that *all* men—take steps toward finding themselves. Some may feel a momentary relief that such a men's movement has taken off. I know, as I've already said, that there are men who really are examining their history, culture, their patterns of behavior. On the other hand, we've long been programmed to applaud the initiatives of men, however shallow or short-lived. Some of us are immensely tired of the rantings, but hardly moved to respond.

Except for one important consideration. Today's media, by its intent and capabilities, engenders immediate and widespread reproduction of those ideologies, such as Bly's, that safeguard power. The Reagan and Bush administrations have provided a succession of lessons in how this can be done. Witness the erasure of the Vietnam era's reexamined morality, leading to an acceptance of the invasion of one sovereign nation after another and culminating in yellow ribbon–bedecked cheering over the U.S.-led massacre in the Persian Gulf. Witness the language of Western fundamentalism, how it has succeeded in whipping emotions to a frenzy around such euphemisms as "the right to life." Consider how easily and relatively painlessly, in our government's rhetoric, contras become "freedom fighters," affirmative action becomes quotas. Today newscasters are busy making sure we understand that only we can end the economic recession. We and the Japanese (if only they would behave correctly). All we need is something called *consumer confidence*. Translated into the language of everyday living, this means we are being encouraged to spend more money, buy more things—even as our jobs are taken from us and our social services reduced to mere shadows of their former selves.

When the media focuses on one aspect of the "men's move-ment," especially at a time when terms like "the death of feminism" or "postfeminist era" are so in vogue, we do well to ask a few questions about what the "theories" really say. What is the "take home message?" *Iron John* is an easy place to begin. The very first sentence lays bare its deepest fallacy: "[T]he images of adult manhood given by the popular culture are worn out; a man can no longer depend on them."[4] What Bly avoids throughout his rather convoluted treatise is any recognition of the fact that our popular culture is itself an eminently male creation.

Bly's basic premise is that women, in our reclamation of memory and in the process of taking back our power, have left men fumbling. Being blamed, of course, is nothing new to us. But if we stop right here and examine the accusation, we may be able to remind ourselves of our own intrinsic selfhood, stop taking on the burden. Bly speaks of "soft men" and with his "some-of-my-best-friends-are" manner, even claims to be fond of them. "They're lovely, valuable people—I like them," he says. But wait. After conceding that such men are "not interested in harming the earth or starting wars," he tells us they "are not happy."[5]

Not because the male-inherited dominant culture stigmatizes "soft" men. Not because our male-produced political culture only rewards those who conquer, rape, maim, kill. Not because capitalism itself is built upon the ravages of to-the-death competition. No. Bly blames women for men's unhappiness. "The strong or life-giving women who graduated from the sixties, so to speak, or who have inherited an older spirit, played an important part in producing this life-preserving, but not life-giving, man."[6]

Bly turns to pre-Christian myth as he urges men to get back in touch with the "Wild Man" within. He evokes images of a "hairy John" baptizing Jesus. "The key," he says, "is under our mother's pillow. . . . Mothers are intuitively aware of what would happen if [their sons] got the key: they would lose their boys. . . . My son the doctor. My son the Jungian analyst. My son the Wall Street genius." Again and always it's the woman's fault. Bly tells us modern man is "too close to the mother's pillow and the father's book of rules."[7]

For this guru is careful to give some lip service to blaming the father as well. At least the father raised by women, the father who has not noticed, in our Rambo-plagued society, that men are "too soft." Sometimes men are to blame by not standing up to castrating women; sometimes the male gender is included like an afterthought, such as in the second half of this sentence: "The possessiveness that mothers typically exercise on sons—*not to mention the possessiveness that fathers typically exercise on daughters. . . .*" (emphasis mine) Or "only men can initiate men, as only women can initiate women."[8]

But what about the possessiveness mothers may exercise on daughters, or fathers may exercise on sons? That's beyond Bly's thought process, which never scratches so far beneath the surface. He has constructed a grotesquely one-dimensional, easily popularized pseudoanalysis guaranteed to appeal to men trained to forget their own history and conditioned to blame their lack of sense of self on *the other:* women. After all, we live in a society where *Women Who Love Too Much* is an instant best-seller, while *Men Who Hit Too Much* has yet to be written.

Heterosexism is also a part of Bly's scheme of things. In his preface he assures us that although "[m]ost of the language in [his] book speaks to heterosexual men [it] does not exclude homosexual men. . . . The mythology . . . does not make a big distinction between homosexual and heterosexual. . . ."[9] Not true. Mythology is the reproduction of values, and our culture certainly places a different, inferior, value on that which is homoerotic, homosexual, pertaining to the love between those of the same sex.

But where the mythology may leave some room for interpretation, Bly himself imposes his rugged heterosexism. Here he extrapolates from a Keith Thompson essay in which a clan of she-wolves runs through the forest, eventually arriving at a riverbank: "Each she-wolf looked into the water and saw her own face there. But when Keith looked in the water, he saw no face at all." Bly, true to form, does not take this to mean that Keith was incapable of seeing himself within a group of strong female images. Rather, he concludes that "Dreams are subtle and complicated. . . . The last image. . . suggests a disturbing idea. When women, even women with the best intentions, bring up a boy alone, he may in some way have no male face, or he may have no face at all[!]."[10]

Bly calls on Sigmund Freud and James Hillman and Michael Meade and Keith Thompson and Robert Moore. Rarely is there a woman's name on his list of mentors of creative spirits. *Iron John* is filled, as well, with references to Rembrandt, Shakespeare, Picasso, Kafka. Bly quotes the psychologist Alice Miller, but the twist he gives to her vision reminds me of the way the Bible or a bourgeois history text is frequently used: to prove any "theory," no matter how absurd.

But it is where Bly draws larger political conclusions that he becomes most pseudoscientific, least reliable, and—I believe—most dangerous. His claim that "the love unit most damaged by the Industrial Revolution has been the father-son bond"[11] not only ignores our history of the exploitation of women and child labor; it neatly prepares us for his ultraconservative views on rebellion and resistance.

According to Bly, "The son's fear that the absent father is evil contributed to student takeovers in the sixties [!]. . . . The students' fear that their own fathers were evil was transferred to all male figures in authority. A university, like a father, looks upright and decent on the outside, but underneath, somewhere, you have the feeling that it and he are doing something demonic. . . ."[12] While women are remembering that fathers and institutions have indeed done much that is demonic, Bly has men *fearing* this may be so!

The son *fears;* he does not *know.* The implication, of course, is that this is all a matter of the son's imagination, an imagination led astray by strong women. Women, of course, in this man's version of history, did not take part in the struggles of the sixties. This is typical of Bly's paternalistic and condescending disregard for the remembering accomplished today through painful hard work by so many women, and also some men.

In fact Bly, like promoters of the poverty-builds-character or abuse-makes-art doctrines, nurtures sickness itself as a source of power. "[W]here a man's wound is," he says, "that is where his genius will be. Wherever the wound appears in our psyches, whether from alcoholic father, shaming mother, shaming father, abusing mother, whether it stems from isolation, disability, or disease, that is precisely the place for which we will give our major gift to the community."[13] And he lists Eduard Munch, Franz Kafka, Charles Dickens, and others as examples of disabling anxiety producing artistic gifts.

Indeed, abuse is present in many creative lives; tragically, it seems to be present in *most* lives, creative or not. But it is not the mere presence of abuse that signals creativity. It is the degree to which we are able to recognize and overcome its paralyzing effects that frees us to make and do.

Iron John bears careful reading. The ways in which Bly plays with reality, the ways he skims the surface of certain truths, twisting them slightly so that the road to discovery is blocked, are both what is so seductive and so threatening about his ideas. For, whatever his rhetoric to the contrary, what Bly really advocates is a world where women are paper-thin pieces of landscape, where men are strong and hairy and unthreatened, and where the following story is appreciated by all:

"[T]he King said . . . I am in debt to you. Whatever I have in my power that would please you, I will give. Well, the young man said, I'd suggest that you give me your daughter as my wife. Then the King's daughter laughed and said, I like the way he doesn't beat around the bush. . . . And so she walked over and kissed him. . . ."[14] This is the story with which Bly ends his book. The message is clear: Men will be okay if women will just stop being so strong; women will be okay as long as men are okay. Do we need further proof of where such "theories" lead?

Notes

1. Carolyn G. Heilbrun, *Writing a Woman's Life* (New York, Norton, 1988).
2. Bill Moyers' Public Broadcasting System's special, "A Gathering of Men," aired in most U.S. cities in the winter of 1990.

3. Robert Bly, *Iron John: A Book About Men* (Reading, MA: Addison-Wesley, 1990).
4. *Iron John*, p. I.
5. Bly, pp. 2–3.
6. Bly, p. 3.
7. Bly, pp. 8–13.
8. Bly, pp. 12–16.
9. Bly, p. x.
10. Bly, p. 17.
11. Bly, p. 19.
12. Bly, p. 21–22.
13. Bly, p. 42.
14. Bly, p. 258.

MARGARET RANDALL *is a writer, photographer, and teacher who lives once again in her native New Mexico after many years in Latin America (Mexico, Cuba, Nicaragua). In 1989 she won a lengthy battle with the U.S. Immigration and Naturalization Service after it tried to deport her because of opinions expressed in her work. She has been teaching the spring semester at universities and colleges around the country, most frequently at Trinity in Hartford, Connecticut. Recent books include* Walking to the Edge: Essays of Resistance *and* This is About Incest.

Nicole Hollander

Men's Predicament:
Male Supremacy

Harriet Gill

As a longtime feminist, I find the new men's movement encouraging, interesting—yet problematic. I see that some men are making efforts to become more conscious, even attempting an acquaintance with their own soul. I try to understand the goal of the movement from what the media, the documentaries, the books, and the workshops are saying about it. My research leads me to this conclusion: The road men are taking toward the goal of liberation has but one obstacle that will prevent them from reaching the mark of transforming growth we call liberation; that obstacle is male supremacy.

While men are indeed reaching for a new sense of what being a man today could mean, I do not see that these efforts include a wish to share real power with women, or to rise to full equality with women. A stunningly practical example of such sharing comes from Professor Robert McElvaine, who suggested recently that one of our country's biggest strongholds of power be shared: by reserving half the seats in Congress for women! The fact that this image is so startling indicates how far men are from a willingness to truly share power.

Male supremacy is the assertion and the silent assumption by men that man is superior to woman. This belief, from phallus worship to the worship of an omnipotent Father God, has justified the oppression and exploitation of women throughout history. It establishes and defends a pervasive double standard: legal, social, economic, philosophic, religious, moral. Because men are immersed in this tacit sense of superiority, they do not look at it or see it for what it is. It does not occur to them to do so, and if it did, I do not know whether they would wish to.

Male supremacy demands a serious and persevering analysis of what it means to men, what positions it forces them into, how the very privilege it gives them at the same time exacts a great price. Robert Bly has said, "Talking of reality is iron." Where in the world is that iron that will bring men to look at the male supremacy in which they live? How can they discover that male supremacy itself lies at the base of their predicament?

The hidden message in the men's movement today is, in effect, "We men will retain our superior power, even increase it. In the meantime, we will find ways to 'true manhood.'" This is what I see as the stance of both Robert Bly and Sam Keen, two widely read spokesmen in the vanguard of the new movement. In the context of male supremacy, what can "true manhood" possibly mean? I say again that without looking at the superior power arrogated by men, given to them by their worldwide cultural inheritance, without studying its effects on women, children, the earth, and men themselves—this movement will change nothing. Instead, it will merely create some new design of male privilege.

All the materials for thought and action being offered men today—philosophy, poetry, mythology, processes that encourage feeling and intuition—are useful, but do not present the reality in which we live. Male privilege continues to cloud men's vision. Until men ask themselves, "In what ways do I exploit women, put them down, ignore them?" and then move from there to find new understanding, new ways to behave, the men's movement will continue to sleepwalk.

A man trying to understand male supremacy in greater depth and to forge new ways of being would do well to add to his reading some books that appeared in the early 1970s discussion of men's liberation. Men speaking for the movement of that time, who were studying men's psyche and behavior, had been inspired by the women's movement. They opened their thinking to what women were telling them of their experiences as they lived their lives—the insult, humiliation, fear, and contempt that women face in the world of male privilege. Given the suffering and pain women were describing, these men sought conclusions about what they must learn and do in order to change society. Current literature avoids this practical approach to confronting male supremacy.

In *Iron John*, Robert Bly faults those men who listened and responded to women; he says men became "soft," and insists that softness cannot equal true masculinity. This feminist way, according to Bly, is not going to help men to know true manliness. That lies elsewhere. The way to manhood is through warriorhood, the ability to be fierce. Although Bly attempts to differentiate between the warrior tempered by tenderness and the "savage," many have responded negatively to this word with its military implication, and certainly the word can easily be misunderstood by women living under the threat and reality of male violence.

Just how warriorhood is to be expressed and then disciplined is not clear. Bly's book is full of poetry and mythic stories that capture the mind, and can be very stimulating for those who haven't been exposed to mining the psychological meaning in fairy tales and myths. However, its vagueness will keep it from becoming a transforming book for men, as Simone de Beauvoir's *Second Sex* was for women. An experiential clarity is needed. Perhaps Bly's workshops provide this.

I turned to Sam Keen's *Fire in the Belly* with hope and interest. In the first part of this book, Keen tells us how he found that "fire in the belly" as he faced the necessity of ending his relation with a much younger woman that began soon after his divorce. This story illustrates my contention that Keen is unaware of how he is caught in the thrall of male supremacy. All the many good things he has to say lose force because they are in the shadow of this thrall, and he does not know it. He tells the story:

To free himself from the need for this woman, he walked the hills of San Francisco on an extended drunk until his "being turned liquid." He chooses this moment to phone her (she has already rejected him more than once) and says grandly: "I know it is time for you to go. As much as I want to be with you, I know there is no way for us to remain lovers. I am too old and too raw to be casual about love, and you are too young to be faithful and make graceful commitments. Go without deception or guilt. I love you. Goodbye."

I appreciate Keen's honesty, but I find the story romanticized fiction. Who is he to say what her capabilities for commitment are when his own marriage has recently ended? He confesses as well to quickly starting another affair as he began to grow insecure with this younger woman. This story sets the tone for the unconscious male privilege that is everywhere expressed in his book.

Another example: Suffering after his divorce, Keen seeks the counsel of his mentor, Rev. Howard Thurman, who tells him: "There are two questions a man must ask himself. First, 'Where am I going?' and second, 'Who will go with me?'" Keen says that this counsel was the most important bit of advice he ever got about being a man. These questions proclaim that the life that is to be lived in marriage will be the man's life. But does Keen know, has he heard, that many women today are asking: "Where is my own journey, my own fulfillment?" While he claims to be aware of the contemporary status of women, Keen seems to reject the most vital part of feminist thinking where he would find this included.

Keen includes in his book a set of questions that men can ask themselves in order to know where they presently stand. Included are the following: What pleasures and privileges do you enjoy as a man? What is hardest about being a man? If pursued, these two questions might open a man's serious thinking to what male privilege means to him. Male supremacy is hidden especially in that question, "What is hardest about being a man?" Keen's questions can be useful if answered in depth, but as stated they cover too much ground. I have some questions myself, but mine are more specific.

I would ask men to examine their personal definition of themselves. For example, a man could ask: "Why do I think sexual harassment of women is my right? Has it ever occurred to me that I think this way? Am I uncomfortable in the face of female authority? Why? Does my attitude toward women in the workplace need to change? Why do I think that what I do and say is more important than what women do and say? Why do I monopolize conversations with women, leaving them practically no space to respond? Why do I without a second thought expect personal service from women—housework, cooking, child care, valet service, erranding? Why do I expect a woman to defer to me, to give me the lion's share of the speaking time, and more coddling than I deserve? Do I ever think of sharing my prerogative of making the first social move? Why am I so often taciturn, unresponsive, dour, unlistening? Why is it that I do not take women seriously? How am I unfair, hard-hearted, even cruel? In what ways do I exploit women? How can I change these things about myself? Do I wish to? Have I been justifying my exploitation of women?" These questions could help men look male supremacy squarely in the eye.

To speak of men as though they constitute a monolith would be misleading. We all share attributes that make up human character. Some men are sweet, patient, and kind, as some women are not. But what has descended on all of us is an automatic expectation that a man's behavior will act out his male-supremacist assumptions and that a woman will respond in the fact of them, depending on the painful learning and unlearning she has gone through.

In my own response to male supremacy, I ask myself to look at it carefully. I live surrounded by it. I can respond to it in a number of ways: accepting, adapting, avoidance, withdrawal, not noticing, or straight-on confrontation. Within me there is fear, constricted ideas of where I can go, what I can do, and what I can say. The confidence that is part of my temperament has been in the past pushed to the wall by male supremacy. It lives again and grows in the nurturance of the women's movement and its sisterhood.

Perhaps only a fraction of the men in this country have joined the new men's movement. It may be that these are the very ones who have felt the strain of their privilege. And there is a larger fraction of men who have begun to notice what they are doing and thinking, and realize they can no longer claim innocence of the effects of their privilege. They have known this a long while, but haven't had the interest, time, or pressing need to investigate it further. At best, perhaps this new movement indicates that something has awakened in them that has always been there: a questioning of the assumptions by which they have lived.

Is the men's movement today a movement? Perhaps it might best be called an occasional manifestation. It has the elements of a fad: a great deal of attention paid for a while and then forgotten, just as the men's movement of the 1970s seems to exist now only in books. A true movement springs up spontaneously everywhere, as did the liberation movements for blacks and women, and then perseveres to change society's fundamental assumptions.

"What is the use of being a little boy if you have to grow up to be a man?" asked Gertrude Stein. Underneath this cryptic remark is a call to men to look at their assumed entitlements. As hopeful and encouraging as the men's movement is, male supremacy—unstudied and unchallenged—will keep men from moving ahead. It lies with men to face how male supremacy informs every aspect of their lives, and what it means in their relationships to women, children, other men, and to the earth.

Born before women had the vote, HARRIET GILL has been a feminist since she was nine years old. It was then she realized "something was wrong." Finding her first consciousness-raising group in

Berkeley in 1966 was a turning point in her life. She has been in the women's movement for twenty-five years. Harriet is a clinical social worker whose work since 1941 has been helping people with life problems. For five years on KPBS, the public radio station in San Diego, she has broadcast weekly essays on all aspects of living. Besides the serious study of feminism and its history, she is a student of world affairs, music, art, and architecture. It was her interest in the latter that led her to found Friends of San Diego Architecture seven years ago. She is the director of this grass-roots organization that brings together lay and professional people for monthly lectures and discussion of architecture and design. At seventy-eight, her latest effort to remain joined to the human race is strength training!

Beauty and the Beast:
A Parable for Our Time

Elizabeth Dodson Gray

ROBERT BLY AND the men's movement in its mytho-poetic form is totally focused on myth and story as meaning. So it seems appropriate to focus upon a story as a lens through which to examine the men's movement. "Beauty and the Beast" is an old fairy tale that has recently been powerfully recast in movie form.

A Mythopoetic Tale

Beauty in the movie is a daringly different girl. She is full of life and energy, and in love with reading (she has a mind!). She dreams of a wider world not seen by the villagers and yet disparaged by them. In the movie Beauty magically has no mother but is totally devoted to her father. Beauty is also easily able to discern that the arrogant but handsome Gaston is a macho fluffhead.

The village where Beauty and her father live is fully populated with typical patriarchal values, and the center of attention in the movies is the Beast. The Beast, living in isolation in his castle, is really a male under a spell. He is not himself but is ugly on the surface. And he has a terrible temper. Does the Beast's psychological profile in the film remind you of a violence prone wife batterer? Hmm!

And the story line? Beauty sacrifices herself to save her father's life. She then feels called upon to sacrifice herself again, this time to save or redeem the Beast. The spell that is upon the Beast is broken "by the love of a good woman," and Beauty frees him finally to become his concealed wondrous self. The movie retells the story behind the T-shirt caption, "To find Prince Charming you have to kiss a lot of toads."

All this is a typical patriarchal tale about what is required of the good woman. She is to sacrifice herself for a man. What is exceptional about "Beauty and the Beast" is the additional condition of the Beast's release, that he is to "genuinely love another."

Common Themes in the Movie and the Men's Movement

What reminded me of the men's movement was that while Beauty gets cobilling in the story title and movie, the whole focus is really upon the Beast. The central question is, "Will the Beast be delivered from his enchantment? Will he be returned to his true identity?" This focus on the Beast, the male, is shared by the Robert Bly contingent of the men's movement. The central question for them is the redemption of the male from his enchantment by a journey that is the man's perennial quest for his true identity.

In the movie and in the men's movement, the old macho hero is dead. Robert Bly and Sam Keen and others are clear that the true male self is not the Gaston of the movie. Gaston in the movie is clearly the outdated male stereotype: handsome, arrogant, athletic, conceited, macho, and attracted to Beauty only by her physical appearance.

The old macho hero may be dead, but the Beast is still with us. In "Beauty and the Beast" there is the clear mythopoetic representation of the man who is totally preoccupied with his own salvation, who is prone to violence, and who is still very much "under the spell" of an enchantment. While he was living his life and occupying his own niche or slot within the patriarchal system, he was overcome, captured, transformed in his being, "enchanted." What is unsaid (and unseen) is that it is indeed the patriarchal system of relationships that has done this to him and that has transformed his life, making him into the Beast.

We glimpse this man also in the men caught up by the Robert Bly portion of the men's movement, men who are the audience for his best-selling book *Iron John*.[1] They are men desperately searching for the salvation of their male souls. Their quest is for the Holy Grail of a "primal" masculinity. But sadly what these men (and Bly) do not yet perceive is the true cause of their enchantment. They do not yet grasp what it is that holds them captive, namely the patriarchal system itself.

According to the mythopoetic men's movement, each man seeks, and Robert Bly offers, an individual journey of salvation. What they do not yet understand is that this is impossible unless they break the spell that holds them captive; and that this spell is not individual and personal but instead organizational and cultural, comprising the entire system of male power and privilege and violence that feminists have named "patriarchy."

Bly himself does not understand this. While he says he eschews the macho male of the past, Bly's foundational myth of "Iron John" is taken from the Brothers Grimm's collection of fairy tales, which arose out of our patriarchal past.

Honoring Men's Sacred Spaces

While I perceive grievous flaws in Robert Bly's mythology and bemoan his lack of any feminist analysis of male power in the culture, I feel I must also honor what happens in a talking-stick circle. As a woman and a feminist, I know it to be a sacred space when women gather to tell their own stories. I can light a candle to celebrate this as a sacred space. So when men gather in a circle not to talk of football or how many notches they have on their shooter but to talk instead of their own interior life so long concealed and coerced by a John Wayne model of manhood, then I think I must also honor as sacred these spaces being created by men.

The Place of Repentance in Men's Sacred Work

What I want for men is that they be able to find again their interior lives which for so long have been largely ignored by them. It is true that only men are going to be able to redefine masculinity, and shape it into new personal and cultural formulations that are not woman-hating. Robert Bly does not do it. Sam Keen begins it. And as men do it, it is sacred work.

Men's healing themselves must be done within a fundamental repentance for the essential male centeredness of the past. Gus Kaufman is right in his critique of the Bly movement: "Its defect is that it never challenges, never even sees, the most fundamental problem of the construction of manhood: *the assumption of male centrality.* It therefore reproduces patriarchy."[2]

All of us, both male and female, have been socialized into "Adam's World"[3]—there is a major conceptual trap that confuses being human with being male. Men must discover and accept that they are not the center and fullness of the human world, but rather are bipolar partners within this human species. They are but half the human race.

Therefore, while men work out their own salvation with fear and trembling, it must not be done at the expense of women. They must see, understand, and change what they have done to their mothers, wives, sisters, and daughters. And even while they are grieving the wounds they carry as sons of absent and nonfeeling or deriding fathers, they must face up to the present task of being very different fathers for their own sons and daughters.

Rewriting Patriarchal Scripts

Both Bly and Keen assume men can only find themselves by "leaving their mother's household." This is the old patriarchal script of masculinity being named only *in opposition to anything female.* If women are soft, the men must be hard. If women are nurturing, then men must not nurture. And on and on. All this continues the old patriarchal sense that boys are somehow deeply contaminated by their mother's child rearing. What is missing here is a grasp of how it is patriarchy which forces women to do all that child rearing, even as patriarchy is coercing most men to avoid it.

Bly also never examines patriarchy's role in scripting men to overwork. This pattern of overworking causes men to neglect their children and to wound their daughters as well as their sons. Nor is Bly clear about the role of patriarchy as a systemic repressive phenomenon, causing boys and men to bury their feelings and become remote father figures who cannot express love.

Bly apparently does not see how, generation after generation, patriarchy has coerced us all so that men are reared by women, ignored by fathers, and then want to flee women in order to "discover their true masculinity." These social roles that patriarchy designs, coerces, and perpetuates *cause* the very inner wounds Bly describes so eloquently and seeks to heal.

Bly tries nobly to lance men's inner wounds. But he does not perceive their root cause in the power system of patriarchy. So he is helpless to interrupt this process as the generations roll on.

Women's Part in Breaking the Enchantment of Patriarchy

There is a further aspect of "Beauty and the Beast" that delights me. In the story, the release of the Beast from his enchantment can only be accomplished by Beauty, "by the love of a good woman." I find that I can read this role for women in either of two ways. If I think of Beauty sacrificing herself for the beast (as she did for her father), it seems like a nasty replay of patriarchal scripts exploiting women into endless self-denial and self-sacrifice. But on the other hand, if I imagine that this Savior role gives to women—and *only* to women—the power to "break the enchantment" of patriarchy, then that appeals to me.

In the Hindu tradition there is a wonderful story about the Savior role of a goddess named Durga. She is a young and beautiful woman at the height of her sexual powers. Durga comes riding into a world of chaos on the back of a tiger. She saves the day by slaying with her powerful sword the wild boar who is threatening every-thing with disaster.

Durga is a female Savior who is sexual, powerful, and virtuous all at once. Now that is a role for women that I think many of us can identify with. *The Durga myth suggests it is only feminism that has the power to lift the spell of patriarchy.*

Patriarchy as a New Jericho

I often visualize patriarchy as a castle (much like the one in "Beauty and the Beast") standing high on a forbidding hill, an entrenched system of male power and privilege protecting fragile men living inside its defended walls and wide moats. I also visualize the work of feminist women as being like that of Joshua, marching around those defended walls (in the Hebrew Scriptures, Jos. 6:1–21). We are blowing our trumpets of the feminist critique of male culture, marching and blowing, marching and blowing, seven times around, even seventy times around, until the walls of our Jericho come tum-bling down.

The enchantment of patriarchy requires a feminist analysis of cul-ture to dissolve, something the profeminist wing of the men's move-ment understands all too well. The profeminist men understand that *a men's movement that is centered only upon men and only promale, and only looks at the costs of masculinity (i.e., the costs of patriarchy to men), can never break its own enchantment.*

To free ourselves from patriarchy, we must all become profemale and look at the costs *to women* of male power, male privilege, and male violence. It is also equally true that to free ourselves of racism, we can never just look at the costs to whites but we must identify with the true costs to African-Americans of white power, privilege, and violence. So I see feminism as leading the way in a cultural procession of conceptual Aha's—the breaking of evil enchantments as in "The Emperor has no clothes!"

I would invite into our procession around the walled city of patriarchy all those whose lives are emerging out of the cultural myths of the past and coming into new and liberating identities which are expressions of their own uniqueness.

I invite to join us all women who are increasingly claiming their power to name themselves, and are finding that in their renaming they change their world. Patriarchy has been a prison for women that none of us any longer need.

I would also open our ranks to all those women who suddenly understood while watching the Clarence Thomas hearings that sexual harassment, rape, date rape, pornography, battering, and violent death for women are part and parcel of patriarchal male power. I would welcome all those women who learned anew that within patriarchy "a woman will not be believed."

Feminism—recognition of the imbalance of power between men and women, combined with a commitment to correct that imbalance—is the only solvent that will dissolve patriarchy and release all of us, women and men, from its power.

But I also want to open our ranks to all the children who care about their future on this endangered planet. Patriarchy is a root cause of "ranking diversity." It is the conceptual basis for male domination over and exploitation of "lesser" genders, peoples, races, species, and of nature and the planet itself. Patriarchy is thus a conceptual cancer that is simply not compatible with the health of our interconnected Earth-system.[4]

And finally I open the ranks of our marchers to men. We can welcome all the men who can finally touch their feelings, name their wounds, and look in new places for the core of their positive male energy, as Sam Keen does in his book *Fire in the Belly*.[5]

Men Challenging Men to End Violence Against Women

I like Sam Keen's book very much because Keen says that male identity and virility in *this* historical time is found in a new vocation to save the planet. But it is distressing to me that neither Sam Keen's book nor Robert Bly's *mention* the epidemic of male violence against women. That omission seems to me like building a boat (a new sense of male identity) in a thunderstorm and never mentioning the thunderstorm! Or it is like focusing on the feelings of S.S. guards while the ovens of genocide burn a few feet away. It is like pondering the feelings of white people while black people are being lynched just over the hill.

For men challenging men to end violence against women, we must look to the profeminist men within the men's movement. These are the men who have focused upon trying *as men* to stop the male violence against women. The White Ribbon Campaign in Canada was organized by such men. The campaign focuses around the second anniversary of the Montreal Massacre of women when twenty-five-year-old Marc Lepine denounced "feminists" as he shot fourteen women dead in a rampage at the Ecole Polytechnique.

The campaign was thought up by three men (Ron Sluser, Jack Layton, and another) but joined by other prominent Canadian men including Senator Trevor Eyton, environmentalist David Suzuki, and actor Bruno Gerussi. They were very clear about the need *for men* to accept responsibility for both male violence to women and for trying as men to stop it.

These are excerpts from the text of their 1991 "White Ribbon" statement:

> *If it were between countries, we'd call it a war. . . . But it's happening to women, and it's just an everyday affair. It is violence against women. It is rape at home and on dates. It is the beating or the blow that one out of four Canadian women receive in their lifetime. It is the sexual harassment at work and sexual abuse of the young. It is murder.*
>
> *There's no secret enemy pulling the trigger. No unseen virus that leads to death. It's just men. Men from all social backgrounds and of all colors and ages. Men in business suits and men in blue collars. . . . Just regular guys.*
>
> *All those regular guys, though, have helped create a climate of fear and mistrust among women. Our sisters and our mothers, our daughters and our lovers can no longer feel safe in their*

homes. At night they can't walk to the corner for milk without wondering who's walking behind them. . . . Even the millions of women in relationships with that majority of men who are gentle and caring feel they cannot totally trust men. All women are imprisoned in a culture of violence.

Men have been defined as part of the problem. But we are writing this statement because we think men can also be part of the solution. Confronting men's violence requires nothing less than a commitment to full equality for women and a redefinition of what it means to be men, to discover a meaning to manhood that doesn't require blood to be spilled.[6]

I find the White Ribbon Campaign encouraging because it reassures me that it is possible for men to take responsibility for the actions of their own gender. Because men commit the violence, it is men who can stop it.

At the end of Robert Bly's book *Iron John,* the newly revealed baronial king says, "I am Iron John, who through an enchantment became turned into a Wild Man."[7] Any Wild Man who wishes to be free of the evil enchantment must turn away from himself and from a male-centered world and life, and become profeminist enough to care about what is happening to women.

The truth is, you cannot affirm life without affirming women, because women's bodies are the gateway to life for all of the human species. The men's movement, unless it is embracing of women— their health, their safety, and their equality—will never be a way to life for men. Remember, the Beast, to free himself, had to truly love another.

Notes

1. Robert Bly, *Iron John: A Book About Men* (Reading, MA: Addison-Wesley, 1990).
2. Gus Kaufman, Jr., "Healing the Pain by Misplacing Blame: Some Thoughts on the Men's Movement," *Working Together* (newsletter of the Center for the Prevention of Sexual and Domestic

Violence, 1914 North 34th, Suite 105, Seattle, WA 98103) 2:3 (Spring/Summer 1991), p. 8. Emphasis added.

3. Elizabeth Dodson Gray, *Patriarchy as a Conceptual Trap* (Wellesley, MA: Roundtable Press, 1982), pp. 48–49. See also the eighteen-minute film *Adam's World* (1989) by the National Film Board of Canada.

4. See Elizabeth Dodson Gray, *Green Paradise Lost* (Wellesley, MA: Roundtable Press, 1979).

5. Sam Keen, *Fire in the Belly: On Being a Man* (New York: Bantam, 1991).

6. The White Ribbon Campaign: Breaking Men's Silence to End Men's Violence (December 1–6, 1991), 253 College Street, Box 231, Toronto, Ontario M5T 1R5.

7. *Iron John*, p. 259.

ELIZABETH DODSON GRAY *is a feminist theologian, environmentalist, and futurist. Her book* Green Paradise Lost *(1979) had a pioneering role in the development of ecofeminism. She is coordinator of the Theological Opportunities Program at Harvard Divinity School and has taught at MIT's Sloan School of Management, Williams College, Boston College, and Antioch/New England Graduate School. She is also the author of* Patriarchy as a Conceptual Trap *(1982) and editor of* Sacred Dimensions of Women's Experience *(1988). In 1989 the National Film Board of Canada released an eighteen-minute film,* Adam's World, *about her work.*

Treating the Symptoms, Ignoring the Cause

Charlene Spretnak

SEVERAL YEARS AGO the cultural historian Ivan Illich came to the University of California at Berkeley for one semester to present his forthcoming book, *Gender*. Each week he held forth in an open seminar in a large auditorium. At the end of the semester a self-organized panel of respondents, who were female professors from various disciplines, presented critiques that were unmistakably respectful of Illich's earlier books, but challenged much of the assumptions, evidence, and theorizing in the new work. These responses were presented one afternoon to an overflow crowd as Illich became increasingly disconcerted and alternately leapt from his seat in the first row of the audience, strode up the aisle and out the door of the auditorium, then returned and took his seat—for a while. Afterward, I chatted with Laura Nader, a professor of anthropology who had been sitting next to Illich throughout the presentations. Had there been time for her to ask a question at the "open mike" on the floor, she told me, the issue that seemed central to her was this: "Dr Illich, when you turned your attention to institutions, you critiqued the power structure. When you turned your attention to the

169

medical profession, you critiqued the power structure. When you turned your attention to the education establishment, you critiqued the power structure. So, why—when you turned your attention to gender—didn't you critique the power structure?"

Why, indeed. I find Professor Nader's question coming to mind repeatedly as I hear accounts and descriptions of the men's movement. That the privileged sex in our patriarchal society would find their cultural power and position irrelevant to a soul-searching analysis on their part illustrates the very problem feminism has long addressed: Patriarchal culture shapes the socialization of both sexes and also institutionalizes a preference for males and "masculine" values—at the expense of the devalued sex. Today, as before, most members of the privileged sex hold fast to the skewed distribution of power, in spite of a new enthusiasm for airing substantive complaints about some of the negative effects of patriarchal socialization for males. Feminism has broken the silence about unjust gender dynamics, but most of the men's movement—and most men in general—continue to "stonewall" it.

While I do not doubt that stronger father-son bonding, a current focus in the men's movement, would be healthier for both parties, achieving that particular improvement would not alter the fact that a man's life in a patriarchal society is eased at every stage by the cultural denigration of women. The playing field on which they win is definitely not level. In the interest of honesty, men might take inventory of all the ways in which they benefit from the collective oppression of women. Men might consider the following questions, substituting real lives for the well-known statistics.

As boys, you and others were called on more often in school, taken more seriously, and given more encouragement; think about the girls sitting among you in class whose lives were pruned and contained. You and other young men later began to receive awards, grants, contracts, or other opportunities from sources that routinely give only a very small percentage to women; think about your female peers who were shut out cold. Most men enjoy salaries that are plumped up by paying women less for comparable work in both the public and private sector; think about the women in your place of employment—especially the struggling single mothers—who take home less pay than they should. Think about what it means to live in a society in which a man's career is equal in value to a woman's life, as the U.S. Senate confirmation hearings on Clarence Thomas demonstrated; the attitude of the senators and most of the people polled was, "Even if he did harass you and make your life miserable, you surely don't expect us to hinder a man's CAREER because of that!" It was the same refrain that traditionally blocks prosecution of middle-class rapists. Violence against women is epidemic and on the increase; think about the uneasy vigilance that necessarily shapes daily decision of nearly every woman you know. Men's voices carry the authority in our patriarchal culture; think about all the bright, capable women you know—relatives, neighbors, acquaintances—who will never be heard as they deserve to be and who long ago gave up trying.

The point of the above exercise is not to generate guilt, but simply to encourage awareness that the persons who live on the privileged end of the dualism that informs sexism—as with racism, classism, ageism, and homophobia—do so at the sacrifice of others.

It is not fair, however, to claim that the entire men's movement stubbornly ignores the power dynamics in patriarchal gender relations. One branch is actively involved with political responses to the "structural violence" (economic and social) in our society toward women and minorities, as well as addressing the direct, physical violence women face. An example is Real Men, an organization in Cambridge, Massachusetts, an organization that speaks to men's groups about patterns of violence against women and raises money for shelters for battered women. Another example of work within this orientation is the pamphlet for men titled "Overcoming Masculine Oppression in Mixed Groups" by Bill Moyers and Alan Tuttle (available from New Society Publishers in Philadelphia), which has been widely circulated in social-change movements for fifteen years. A second branch resides in academia and focuses on various issues in "men's studies." Another branch, alas, is the "men's rights movement," which is aggressively misogynist and works primarily to influence judicial thought in the area of family law. By far the best-known manifestation of the men's movement, though, is the mythopoetic branch.

The best-known figure in the mythopoetic men's movement is Robert Bly, whose own journey through various explanatory points of view mirrors, to some extent, that of the movement itself. Hence a brief survey of that progression is appropriate as a partial mode of comprehending his following. Noting the growing interest in the history of Goddess religion, Bly turned his attention in the second half of the 1970s to writing and performing poems on that theme— or at least a variation of it. He traveled around the country giving readings that were billed as being simply about the Goddess but that fixated much of the time on the most bloodthirsty versions, his *Teeth-Mother Naked,* for example, which he had published several years before. In doing so, he expressed the common anxiety of men under patriarchy that the elemental power of the female is essentially devouring and rapacious. He showed no interest in research into Goddess forms in prepatriarchal societies because those orientations regarded cycles of creation and destruction as natural rhythms of the sacred whole, rather than murderous rampages by a demonic feminine. The symbol called "vagina dentata," so important to Freud and other patriarchal theorists, has never been found in excavations of nonpatriarchal cultures. Woman the Devourer, in short, is a projection of the patriarchal worldview.

In 1982 Bly launched his effort to employ (patriarchal) mythology and folktales to aid men (under patriarchy). In an interview conducted by Keith Thompson in *New Age* magazine, Bly announced his discovery of "soft men": auditoriums full of young men he encountered who had been rendered too sensitive, too kind, too empathic, and too wimpy by the forces of feminism. As an antidote, Bly issued a call for men to discover the "wild man" within. That widely circulated interview revealed a nonchalant attitude toward male violence against women, a shocking position Bly later moved away from when he expanded his thesis to become the book *Iron John.*

Soon afterward, Bly took a cue from the ritual circles in the grass-roots women's spirituality movement, which had been in existence since the midseventies, and began to teach workshops around the country. In the ritual space created in those gatherings, men spoke frankly of their pain and thereby broadened Bly's own conceptualization of the subject. On one occasion during that period, my women's ritual group spent a weekend in the countryside. As it happened, the fiancé of one of our members spent that same weekend in a Robert Bly workshop nearby, drumming and creating manly ritual in the woods. When he entered our house to pick up his inamorata, the atmosphere was slightly charged, as if the molecules in the room were frozen in awareness that two powerful and compelling orientations were suddenly sharing the same space. What might happen? Actually, nothing much. Somewhat stilted greetings were exchanged, and we all agreed to rendezvous at a country restaurant an hour away by car. At the restaurant, the fiancé, whom we all knew and liked, shared some general information about the weekend workshop, including his rather adamant acceptance of Bly's assertion that very large numbers of men had been rendered "soft" in recent years. I asked him slowly in what I hoped was a neutral voice whether he himself knew any such men. He pondered a while and then replied triumphantly that he had indeed once known a man who fit the description perfectly!

Learning from what he heard in the workshops, Bly partially shifted his focus from blaming feminism to blaming inadequate fathering and lack of mentoring for most of men's pain. Still, in 1990, he once again exhibited the habit of blaming the woman in any situation. In a televised interview with Bill Moyers, Bly spoke of his childhood and his new perception that his mother had fashioned a conspiracy with him in order to cruelly lock out his alcoholic father. Moyers hesitated not a moment before offering a commonsense response: Since alcoholics are known to emotionally withdraw from spouses and offspring, is it not probable that your alcoholic father withdrew from your mother, leaving her to seek emotional warmth wherever she could, such as the relationship with her son? Bly looked surprised, but then allowed that such an explanation might possibly have some validity.

Bly's message, modulated considerably since the 1982 *New Age* interview but still framed with questionable Jungian assumptions, moved beyond the boundaries of the men's movement workshops to best-seller status in 1991 via *Iron John*. In my view, that book represents an admirable progression in some respects, but is highly problematic in many others. The latter are exemplified by Bly's enthusiasm for "Zeus energy" as an image of appropriate male behavior. Zeus?! He was a power-wielding bully who terrorized both mortals and immortals and often sought sexual pleasure through duplicity and rape. Zeus was no mensch. Moreover, it is noteworthy that Bly builds his ruminations about men around a folktale in which the young male must steal a key (a phallic object involved with social power because it locks and unlocks a man-made object, the door a prisoner's cage) from the bed of the mother. This foundational portion of the plot reflects the central motivation for patriarchal culture: (1) in such cultures the elemental power of the female body (the capability to bleed in rhythm with the moon, to grow both females and males from our flesh, and to transform food into milk for the very young) is regarded with fear, envy, and resentment; (2) men fear that if women gain social power *in addition to* our elemental power men will be endangered; and (3) wresting social/cultural/economic power from women is hence deemed crucial for men in patriarchal societies. This is the partial message of the myth Bly has made central to his men's-work for ten years.

I have recently been assured that Bly now sees violence against women as a serious issue. In addition, I was encouraged to see a quotation from him in fall 1991 referring disparagingly to the senators in the Clarence Thomas hearings as "patriarchs" guarding the old order. That kind of progressive development in his thinking deserves applause. But, Robert, here's the bad news: You cannot cure the painful symptoms of patriarchal culture—such as inadequate fathering by emotionally crippled men who were taught to construct their identity by means of reactive and insecure fixations on being not-female—without addressing the causal dynamics of such a cultural orientation.

Ever since the neolithic transformation, when the Earth was desacralized in favor of a sky-god and patriarchal chieftain cultures gradually dominated Europe, Eurocentric societies have turned away from the felt connections between humans and the rest of nature and have regarded the elemental power of the female body, like the larger forces of nature, as potentially chaotic, engulfing, and devouring. Once that kind of acculturation cuts off males from the mother/female and nature, men must compensate for their vulnerability of being disconnected by inventing various institutions that simultaneously safeguard one's autonomy (or the autonomy of one's own group) while controlling others. Defense against "emotional entanglement" becomes a priority. Hence enormous amounts of attention and energy are spent on the hierarchical power dynamics I cited earlier. Hence the tragic alienation that distorts the lives of oppressors as well as those of the oppressed.

Patriarchy is not "natural"; it is a cultural choice. Many non-patriarchal societies have responded not with fear and resentment but with true respect and awe for nature and the elemental power of the female body. For a discussion of both types of social orientation, see *Female Power and Male Dominance* by the anthropologist Peggy Reeves Sanday.

Men shaped by our patriarchal culture will never be able to replace the patriarchal dynamics that harm them—or those that harm women and nature—unless they make a deep and lasting peace with their own physicality, their mother's womb-body, all womb-bodies, the Earthbody, and the sacred whole that is the generative cosmos. Only then will they feel at home and embraced in the universe.

CHARLENE SPRETNAK's *work has contributed to the framing of the women's spirituality, ecofeminist, and Green politics movement. She is author of* States of Grace: The Recovery of Meaning in the Postmodern Age, Lost Goddesses of Early Greece, Green Politics *(with Fritjof Capra), and* The Spiritual Dimension of Green Politics, *and is editor of an anthology* The Politics of Women's Spirituality.

Acknowledgments

My heartfelt gratitude to the following people:

Barbara Moulton of Harper San Francisco, for giving me the opportunity to edit this book, for sharing the full weight of its intensity, for editing with intelligence and speed, and for laughing at all my jokes.

Tom Grady, for his support of this project, and to Clayton Carlson, for his initiating spark.

The contributors, for writing from the heart and meeting unconscionable deadlines with grace and good cheer.

Deborah Brink, for her loving companionship, for opening our happy home to this book and enduring my mood swings as I dealt with the material, and for doing the final proof.

My circle of support in Atlanta—Wendy Belkin, Linda Bryant, Red Crowley, Joanne DeMark, Marlene Johnson, Denise Messina, Lee Sloan, Celeste Tibbets, and Rita Wuebbeler—for their wise counsel during the early stages of the book.

My friends at the Tattered Cover Bookstore in Denver, for their encouragement and research assistance.

The staff of Harper San Francisco, for their customary and unfailing efficiency and enthusiasm.

Kay Leigh Hagan